LEADERSHIP
at Every
LEVEL

Five Qualities of
Effective Classroom, School,
and District Leaders

JANELLE CLEVENGER McLAUGHLIN

Solution Tree | Press

a division of

Solution Tree

555 North Morton Street
Bloomington, IN 47404
800.733.6786 (toll free) / 812.336.7700
FAX: 812.336.7790

email: info@SolutionTree.com
SolutionTree.com

Visit **go.SolutionTree.com/leadership** to download the free reproducibles in this book.

Printed in the United States of America

Library of Congress Cataloging-in-Publication Data

Names: McLaughlin, Janelle Clevenger, author.
Title: Leadership at every level : five qualities of effective classroom,
  school, and district leaders / Janelle Clevenger McLaughlin.
Description: Bloomington, IN : Solution Tree Press, [2022] | Includes
  bibliographical references and index.
Identifiers: LCCN 2021050818 (print) | LCCN 2021050819 (ebook) | ISBN
  9781952812378 (paperback) | ISBN 9781952812385 (ebook)
Subjects: LCSH: Educational leadership. | School management and
  organization.
Classification: LCC LB2806 .M396 2022 (print) | LCC LB2806 (ebook) | DDC
  371.2/011--dc23/eng/20211130
LC record available at https://lccn.loc.gov/2021050818
LC ebook record available at https://lccn.loc.gov/2021050819

Solution Tree
Jeffrey C. Jones, CEO
Edmund M. Ackerman, President

Solution Tree Press
President and Publisher: Douglas M. Rife
Associate Publisher: Sarah Payne-Mills
Art Director: Rian Anderson
Managing Production Editor: Kendra Slayton
Copy Chief: Jessi Finn
Editorial Director: Todd Brakke
Production Editor: Miranda Addonizio
Content Development Specialist: Amy Rubenstein
Acquisitions Editor: Sarah Jubar
Proofreader: Elijah Oates
Cover and Text Designer: Laura Cox
Editorial Assistants: Charlotte Jones, Sarah Ludwig, and Elijah Oates

To my parents, Jay and Janet Clevenger, my very first leaders.

And to my amazing children, Sydney and Evan,
who continue to shape the type of leader I am.

Acknowledgments

This book wouldn't have been possible without all the teachers I've had and worked with throughout my life. I'm thankful for the friends, family, and colleagues who openly shared stories from their own leadership journeys for me to include in this book. A special thank you goes out to the leaders who wrote the introductory stories for my chapters: Mike Kneebone, Mike Earnshaw, Noa Daniel, Bob Dillon, and Sandra Weaver.

Educators are a special group of people who serve and support in many arenas. That encouragement from educators in all realms is what gave me the fortitude to realize this dream.

Solution Tree Press would like to thank the following reviewers:

Derrick Cameron
Teacher
Prairie South School Division
Moose Jaw, Saskatchewan

Leah Gauthier
Director for Curriculum & Instruction
Elmwood Park Community Unit School
District 401
Elmwood Park, Illinois

Jeff Lahey
Assistant Principal
Flower Mound High School
Flower Mound, Texas

Peter Marshall
Elementary School Principal
Halton District School Board
Burlington, Ontario

Jason Ozbolt
Dean of Students
Lockport Township High School
Lockport, Illinois

Jennifer Steele
Assistant Principal
Northside High School
Fort Smith, Arkansas

Ringnolda Jofee' Tremain
PK3–8 Principal
Trinity Basin Preparatory
Fort Worth, Texas

Visit **go.SolutionTree.com/leadership** to download the free reproducibles in this book.

Table of Contents

About the Author

Janelle Clevenger McLaughlin is an education consultant for Advanced Learning Partnerships working with districts across the United States. She is a former curriculum director for Manchester Community Schools in Indiana, where she led the high-ability and response to intervention programming, curriculum development, 1:1 implementation, and professional development initiatives. Prior to that role, Janelle spent fourteen years as a classroom teacher. Her experiences as a consultant range from job-embedded coaching for teachers and administrators to leading reflective collaborations and facilitating action-plan development.

Janelle has a strong belief in the power of education and the role leaders play in building a strong foundation for the organization. She has worked with educational leaders in over twenty-five different states and two countries. She has presented on numerous topics at national and international events.

Janelle holds a bachelor of science degree and a master of arts degree in elementary education from Ball State University. She has obtained further licenses in school leadership from Indiana Wesleyan University and gifted and talented education from Manchester University.

To learn more about Janelle's work, visit www.innovativeeducationsolutions.net or follow @Ms_Mac4 on Twitter.

To book Janelle Clevenger McLaughlin for professional development, contact pd@SolutionTree.com.

Introduction

The role of a creative leader is not to have all the ideas;
it's to create a culture where everyone can have
ideas and feel they're valued.
—Sir Ken Robinson

Some days I step in front of a classroom. Some days I walk into a board room. Then there are the days that I work from my desk at home. But regardless of location, situation, and role, I am a leader.

Leadership is not about title or position but about mindset. Your mindset completely impacts the way you think, act, and respond. Do you have a fixed mindset or a growth mindset? Psychologist Carol Dweck, who is recognized as the authority on mindset, has defined a growth mindset like this:

> In a growth mindset, people believe that their most basic abilities can be developed through dedication and hard work—brains and talent are just the starting point. This view creates a love of learning and a resilience that is essential for great accomplishment. (Dweck, 2006, p. 140)

People with a growth mindset have a readiness to self-evaluate and an awareness of what is happening around them. They are willing to accept feedback, reflect on and learn from it, apply it, and grow. Leaders with a growth mindset are not afraid of accountability but welcome it as part of the growth process. They are ambitious, have a big vision, and believe that what they are doing is important. Jim Taylor (2014), author and psychology professor, defines mindset as "the attitudes, beliefs, and expectations you hold that act as the foundation of who you are, how you lead, and the ways in which you interact with your team." It's that combination that develops into a mindset and determines the type of leader you are.

Having the right mindset applies to leaders at every level. School leaders need to have the middle management perspective as they are leading their buildings and also serving on teams under their district leadership. The mindset they model often carries over into the classroom. Similarly, district-level leaders model their mindset to others on their teams, shaping the overall perspective of the districts. Many teachers don't see themselves as leaders, but they are. They are the leaders to the students in the classroom, to those students and adults they encounter in the hallway, and like it or not, to the stakeholders with whom they interact in the community. Why did you become an educator? I think it's safe to say that most of us became teachers because we wanted to make a difference in the lives of the students we teach. We had a desire to serve them in some way. The best leaders have that servant's heart for all those they lead—and the number of students a teacher impacts each year with this mindset is beyond counting.

Think back to a time when you were a student in your favorite teacher's classroom. What made this teacher your favorite? I bet it wasn't because of the classroom lectures or the daily worksheets you got to do for homework each night. I'm guessing it was more about how he related to you personally or how engaging she made the learning process. Anyone you remember in this way was probably a great teacher.

Exceptional teachers and exceptional leaders all seem to possess the same qualities. I have identified five that are essential. Effective leaders are (1) relational, (2) innovative, and (3) flexible, have (4) high levels of integrity, and are (5) lifelong learners. Naturally, you may be stronger in some of these than others. Fortunately, you can learn and grow in each.

Leadership is really about the head *and* the heart. This book is for educators at every level and in every role—in the classroom, at the building level, and at the district level—to equip and empower them to lead from both the head and the heart. Every person deserves a strong and caring leader, and every leader can continue to grow and learn those lessons to serve well. The best part is that you don't have to wait for someone to make a plan for you, hire the right keynote speaker, or send you to that specific conference. You can determine the path to your own leadership growth.

Too often, leadership happens in silos. Organizations run more smoothly and more successfully when there is a culture of trust and transparency. I first noticed this when I made the move from the classroom to a district administrator position. I began to see a disconnect among teachers, principals, and district-level leaders that often came down to the culture being perpetuated by the top leadership of the district. As I began my consulting work, other educators began sharing similar experiences with me. This culmination of my own career path being echoed in that of others led me to write this book to shed some light on leadership at every level and attempt to eliminate the silos. That is why there are stories, examples, and strategies for each type of leader in every chapter. Some of these stories are my own, some were shared informally throughout my career, and others I actively sought out as I was writing the book. Being able to understand the strategies and processes that go into decision making at each level of education not only helps you lead in your current position but also helps provide insight into the decisions happening daily in the other leadership positions. Look for the following icons in each chapter.

These vignettes highlight leadership from a classroom teacher.

These vignettes highlight leadership from a building administrator, assistant principal, or dean of students.

These vignettes highlight leadership from a district coach, superintendent, or curriculum director.

The first chapter of this book discusses servant leadership and the points of focus leaders need to remember: cultivating trust and empowering others. Chapters 2–6 then each cover one of the five qualities discussed earlier that are essential and necessary to be a true servant leader: (1) relationality, (2) innovation, (3) flexibility, (4) integrity, and (5) lifelong learning. I'd recommend choosing one area to focus on first, and then move to the next quality you want to develop. Each chapter contains a Leadership at a Glance table with practical application of the concepts discussed, giving leaders in all roles a cross-perspective for how to build that leadership quality in the classroom, the school, and the district.

Learning is only beneficial if you do something with it. The leadership action plan document in figure I.1 (page 4) will help you do just that. It is designed for you to complete section by section after reading the accompanying chapter. Use the Resources column to jot down references mentioned in the chapter that you might want to dig into a bit deeper, or other resources that might help you accomplish the action steps. By the end of the book, you'll have a plan already built and ready to implement as you continue your leadership journey.

It's likely that you entered this career to serve a larger purpose. Most teachers know that education won't make them rich and famous—and few go into teaching with those goals in mind but rather with the intent to serve others. Don't get me wrong: as leaders, we all have areas in which we can grow, but we should all have a commitment to that growth as it benefits us, our students, our peers, and our staff members.

Prompt	Action and Reflection	Resources
Spend some time reflecting on your current leadership role. What traits do you possess that enable you to be a better leader? What areas do you feel like you want to improve in? Do a quick write as an initial reflection point.		
Leaders are relational: Write down three ways you currently foster relationships. Next, write down three more strategies you could implement to be more relational. You should be able to enact at least one of these strategies immediately.		
Leaders are innovative: How are creativity and innovation being stifled in you or for your stakeholders? How can you change that?		
Leaders are flexible: Describe a time that you wish you had been more open minded. How will that experience guide you to be a more flexible leader in the future?		
Leaders have integrity: What are your unbendable values and morals? How do they affect your leadership? Write your personal moral code and then reflect on how that plays out in your role as an educational leader.		
Leaders are lifelong learners: How do you learn best? What are you currently reading, listening to, or watching that is helping you be better in your role? Where can you carve out time for intentional learning on a daily basis?		
Putting it into action: After reading this book, and completing this plan, it's time to personalize it even more to be exactly what you need. Write the five traits in the order you want to tackle them. Some might go together, and that's OK. Then, get to work! ☺		

Figure I.1: Leadership action plan.

*Visit **go.SolutionTree.com/leadership** for a free reproducible version of this figure.*

Throughout this book, you will have the opportunity to dive into the individual areas of servant leadership and explore strategies and practices for growth.

The life of an educator is rich in experience but often short on time. The structure of this book takes your time commitments into account; it's broken down into each of the key leadership characteristics with specific questions for reflection at the end of each chapter. It's ideal for book studies; use it in a collaborative team, as a school, or even as an entire district. Some of the deepest learning happens by reflecting with peers.

CHAPTER 1

What Makes an Effective Leader?

I love spending time talking to leaders and picking their brains, even outside the realm of education. Good leadership is good leadership, regardless of industry. Just as good leadership is universal, ineffective leaders often share many of the same characteristics as well and are often summarized by experts under various leadership styles. Author and university professor Steven C. Wynn addresses this point in his 2019 dissertation "What Research Says About Leadership Styles and Their Implications for School Climate and Teacher Job Satisfaction." Wynn (2019) identifies autocratic leadership as a type where decisions are centralized and limited to only the leader's input. These leaders are typically micromanagers, seeming to delegate responsibility, but then making sure everything is carried out to their specifications. This type of leader instills fear rather than a collaborative spirit.

Inversely, Wynn (2019) describes democratic leadership as a style that is more inclusive, where the leader makes decisions based on the input of each team member. He writes, "The leader encourages participation in decision making—either formally through requests for feedback or informally whenever their followers want to engage" (Wynn, 2019). Democratic leaders seek ways to build their teams and show their employees that they are valued and an important part of the organization. These leaders embody a combination of democratic, strategic, and coach-style leadership. The best ones have the most positive characteristics identified in each style, which leads them to be more like servant leaders by nature. *Servant leaders* put the needs of their stakeholders first. They lead alongside those they lead and aren't concerned with individual recognition. In this chapter, we'll explore how servant leadership is the most effective leadership style and how developing five essential qualities can help leaders at every level exemplify servant leadership.

Servant Leadership

In just three years working under an autocratic leader, I saw over tw~
ees resign exclusively because of the leader and the climate he h~

dissertation, Wynn (2019) states, "Teachers become unhappy working in such an environment and job satisfaction suffers." That was clearly the case for this autocratic leader.

Let's see how one of those people who resigned, Carolyn, a seasoned school building leader, remembers her time working for him.

A Look at Leadership in a School

Carolyn, a retired principal, recalls a time in her career working for an autocratic leader. One morning, she had gone over to the central office to get mail. The superintendent called her into his office to discuss a reading initiative at her school. He asked how the conversations with the teachers were progressing, but before she could even share the answer, he began informing her of exactly how he wanted her to lead the initiative. He didn't ask her advice or get the background regarding staff and student buy-in. As a result, Carolyn left the meeting feeling unheard and undervalued. As the leader of the building, she had valuable insight into the needs of her students and how to lead them to success. Her superintendent's leadership style didn't allow room for that insight to be shared.

In this example, you can see how a top-down leadership style at the district level hindered growth at the building level. Carolyn was able to use that experience to shape her own leadership practices in a positive way.

In contrast to this autocratic style of leadership, the best leaders all tend to share similar characteristics. They are servant leaders who cultivate a culture of trust and empower their teams to grow and thrive. Robert K. Greenleaf, well-known businessman and thought leader, first coined the term *servant leaders* in an essay he wrote in 1970 entitled *The Servant as Leader*. In the revised edition of this essay, Greenleaf (2015) says, "The servant-leader is a servant first. . . . Do those served grow as persons? Do they, while being served, become healthier, wiser, freer, more autonomous, more likely themselves to become servants?" (p. 6).

South Carolina ASCD published a blog post in 2019 titled, "Continuing to Shine the Light on Servant Leadership" in which they wrote:

> Good teachers care about and for their students and good principals do the same for their faculty and students. . . . In both contexts, these leaders want to build a community of shared values in which individuals learn to trust and support one another in moving toward, achieving, and surpassing shared goals.

Sometimes, administrators have been disconnected from a classroom community for many years. Just as teachers can learn from their leaders, leaders can learn from their teachers. Take time to visit classrooms with a strong spirit of community, and observe what the teacher does to nurture that culture. Then, spend time reflecting on how you can bring those strategies into your own leadership practice.

Servant leaders have open discussions and value input from the entire team. They have an eye on both operations and growth opportunities. And they build teams where they can rely on specific skills, talents, and interests of individuals. They listen, care, and are innovative in their thoughts and approaches.

Tom, former teacher and principal and now assistant superintendent, has worked with various leaders throughout his career. He has seen a shift in leadership styles since the onset of his days in the classroom.

A Look at Leadership in a District

Tom, an assistant superintendent, notices a change in leadership since his first years in education. What used to be more of a management model has become a more collaborative model. He has seen an increase in trusting and listening and less top-down leadership. More servant leadership has led to an increase in working together, modeling leadership, and communicating expectations more clearly and specifically. These changes are how he models his own leadership style, and he has seen positive effects on school districts as a result.

In this example, an educator with over twenty years of experience as a leader in education has shown how a more democratic leadership style, along with a servant leadership mentality, has shaped the most effective districts. He tailored his own leadership style to reflect those best practices.

Servant leadership has two focus points that must permeate your actions as a leader every day. Before we get into a more detailed discussion of the five leadership qualities, it's important to devote some time to considering the importance of (1) trust and (2) empowering others.

Cultivate Trust

While leaders demonstrate a *type* of leadership, many develop a *philosophy* of leadership as well. For servant leaders, trust is central to their leadership philosophy, and establishing trust requires building strong relationships. Education thought leaders Thomas C. Murray and Eric Sheninger emphasize the importance of trust and relationship building in their 2018 ASCD blog post, "What It Means to Be a True Leader." They write, "Empowerment leads to respect and trust, which builds powerful relationships where everyone is focused on attaining specified goals" (Murray & Sheninger, 2018). Servant leaders don't take over a room. They empower those around them to find their strengths and share them with the group. They realize the needs of those they serve should be above agendas.

Teacher leaders often recognize the need to put their students first. As a high school mathematics teacher, Chris puts relationships before content when he checks on the emotional well-being of one of his students. He quickly realizes the power in servant leadership and how it carries over into the academic lives of his students.

A Look at Leadership in a Classroom

Chris remembers walking into class one day and noticing a girl with her head down. Instead of ignoring her or telling her to sit up, he walked over and asked her how she was feeling. He asked if there was anything he could do for her. She didn't open up or cheer up much, but the next day she came in and told him that it meant so much to her that he didn't just yell at her to pick her head up. From that day on, she was a super positive student in his mathematics class. That one small act built the foundation of a relationship that carried over for the rest of the school year.

The key takeaway from this vignette is that teachers benefit from taking the time to truly foster relationships with students. It only takes a moment of really seeing them, picking up on nonverbal cues, and following up with a quick question to determine their needs. Relationships build trust, which leads to greater buy-in to the rest of the work in the classroom.

As an elementary teacher, I served the students in my classroom. Those students knew I wanted and welcomed them in the classroom every day. They knew that I cared about them and that I would push them to do their best every day. Yes, I knew their reading skills and mathematics abilities. But I also knew how all my students worked in groups, whether they were more introverted or extroverted, what genres they preferred to read, and how organized they were. I knew who they usually played with at recess and who their siblings were. I talked with their parents and learned about their home lives. I did all that through building authentic, trusting relationships with each student. While I no longer teach elementary students, building relationships remains a top priority and is key to the work of teachers, coaches, consultants, and other education leaders.

Similarly, it's vital for school and district leaders to cultivate trust in those they lead. School leaders should take time to connect with each teacher individually, fostering purposeful interaction and demonstrating genuine care. Through these conversations, they can encourage risk taking in the classroom as well. It's important for all education leaders to be visible in the buildings and community. District administrators can cultivate trust simply by modeling the actions they expect. They need to show up in the lunchroom, in classrooms, at school concerts, and at sporting events. This visibility provides for authentic communication with all stakeholders, increasing trust between all parties.

Empower Your Team

Being a servant leader is not a job or a position, and it's more than a style of leadership. Being a servant leader means that the words of the leader match the attitude and actions of the leader. Such leaders strive to inspire and empower others each day. Servant leaders take that goal into the classroom, school building, and office every single day.

Teachers should strive to empower their students daily. They can do that by establishing a safe community that encourages students to take risks and set their own learning goals. Teachers can help students identify their strengths and use them to drive their own growth. Principals need to establish a similar culture so that their teachers feel empowered. They can also help teachers identify personal strengths and give them leadership opportunities around those areas. Principals who are also seen as coaches have built that trust relationship and can empower their teachers to try new things through those coaching conversations. District leaders have the responsibility of empowering their cabinet-level team members, as well as the building-level leaders in the district. Holding open discussions among various groups and staying consistent in communication helps build trust while also empowering others.

Teachers, principals, and district administrators all face universal issues in education daily as they lead with trust and empower those around them. The good news is that leaders can also develop universal qualities to offset or counter the effects of these issues.

Leadership Qualities

What is the most important character trait in a leader? Ask that question to ten different people, and you could possibly receive ten different answers. I always appreciate quotes, tweets, and blog posts that differentiate between leading and managing, between a leader and a boss. I have worked for both. And all those experiences have helped mold my idea of the most important characteristics leaders should possess.

There are so many articles sharing top leadership characteristics. Many cite ten to fifteen different traits that mark top educational leaders. What I have discovered through coaching educational leaders, however, is to narrow the focus for more effective work. Teachers who see fifteen different things to work on or change can feel overwhelmed, which can lead to growth paralysis. By sifting through the various studies, I found five qualities that continually rose to the top. For focused learning and application, I've identified these five key traits found in exceptional leaders. Each of the following chapters in this book is dedicated to unpacking one quality as we take a deep dive into each of these areas.

1. **Relationality:** Beth Schaefer (2015), educational leader at the University of Wisconsin–Milwaukee, says, "Leaders cannot lead unless they understand the people they are leading. . . . An effective leader thus must be able to build relationships and create communities." Top leaders know the importance of building authentic relationships. Relationship building looks different depending on the contexts in which leaders find themselves, but the end result is the same. If I take the time to get to know those I lead, they will trust me more, and I will know how best to help them. This relationship ends up strengthening the entire industry, company, or school system.

2. **Innovation:** In a March 2018 article for *Educational Leadership* magazine, education leaders Joanie Eppinga, Chuck Salina, Suzann Girtz, and David Martinez describe their experiences turning around a high school in Washington. They identify the importance of innovative thinking, writing:

    > The school's leaders changed the risk-aversive culture by encouraging staff to innovate—without fear of reprisal if things didn't go as intended. "Just try something!" became the new motto. Mistakes were framed as opportunities to learn, an integral part of the growth mindset. (Eppinga et al., 2018)

    Leaders keep their vision front and center. To do that, they must be seen as creative, intelligent, and innovative. They must model change as something positive. If a leader has taken time to forge authentic relationships, then their innovative ideas and plans will be better received, owned, and worked toward as a collaborative group process rather than as a top-down initiative. Like Steve Jobs said, "Innovation distinguishes between a leader and a follower" (as cited in Griggs, 2016).

3. **Flexibility:** Matthew Lynch (2020), education consultant, writes about the importance of being a flexible leader in his article, "Effective Education Leaders Are Flexible." He says, "Education leaders need to use this flexibility to become more accessible to the people they lead. . . . Being flexible allows you to be there when your teachers and leadership team need you to the most" (Lynch, 2020). Sometimes you learn more from failing than succeeding. Flexibility and an open mind play into this learning environment. Leaders need to be ready to listen to ideas that may differ from their own, adapt when something doesn't go as planned, and keep an even temper through the process.

4. **Integrity:** In her article, "What Is the Relational Leadership Model?," middle school principal Lindsay Rayner (2020) writes, "Ethical leaders engender trust in the people who depend on them. By establishing trust, leaders are able to convince others to follow them, even if the road ahead is difficult."

Leaders lead through their actions more than their words. So be honest, moral, and dignified. Most people can tell when their leader is insincere. Without trust, the leadership has no strength.

5. **Lifelong learning:** Northeastern University's Graduate School of Education shares the thoughts of its assistant dean of academic and faculty affairs, Karen Reiss Medwed, in a blog post titled "Three Elements of Educational Leadership" (Knerl, 2019). Medwed says, "A personal commitment to lifelong learning is vital to succeeding in an educational or organizational leadership role. . . . Making lifelong learning a personal priority gives educational leaders the authenticity to share its value to others" (as cited in Knerl, 2019). All leaders must see the importance of continual growth. This commitment starts with each individual. Leading education expert Michael Fullan (2008) writes in *The Six Secrets of Change*, "Avoid superficial learning and instead embed philosophies and principles of learning in the specific contexts that need improvement" (p. 87). Leaders need ongoing professional development, but it must be relevant and authentic to them. Self-assessment to identify areas of passion, interest, and need will help drive goal setting and action steps. Then, regular and intentional reflection must be a part of the learning process to maintain this progress.

Figure 1.1 visualizes these qualities, all five of which effective leaders hold. The circle shape helps emphasize that each of the qualities is on equal footing and should be continuous.

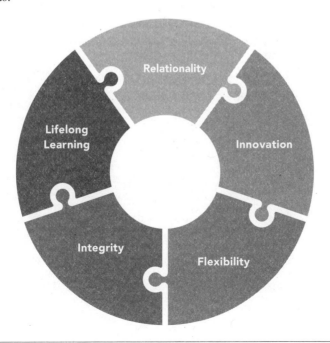

Figure 1.1: Five key qualities found in exceptional leaders.

Table 1.1 shares actions of effective leaders at the classroom, school, and district levels.

Table 1.1: Leadership at a Glance—Actions of Effective Leaders

Focus Point	Leadership in a Classroom	Leadership in a School	Leadership in a District
Cultivate trust.	Cultivating trust in the classroom begins on day one. • Ask questions and listen to your students. • Discover their interests and find ways to bring those into the learning.	School leaders can cultivate trust by fostering purposeful interaction. • Connect with each teacher individually. • Encourage risk taking by inviting ideas and feedback.	Cultivating trust at the district level comes largely through visibility. • Communicate regularly and consistently with all stakeholders. • Model the actions you expect in the district. • Show up in classrooms, at schools, and at extracurricular events.
Empower your team.	Students need to feel like they matter to you and to the class as a whole. • Establish a community. • Encourage risk taking. • Identify individual strengths.	Principals can empower their teams by giving them responsibilities. • Establish a coaching relationship with each person. • Identify individual strengths and help them grow.	District leaders empower their teams in much the same way as building leaders. Additionally, they can do the following. • Hold open discussions. • Validate efforts and guide when necessary.

Questions for Growth and Reflection

The following questions offer an opportunity to reflect on this chapter's content and think about what you might be able to work on.

1. What is one thing you can commit to try to cultivate trust?

2. What do you need from your leaders to feel like you trust them?

3. When do you feel most empowered?

4. Which leadership quality do you feel most confident in?

5. Which leadership quality do you feel like you have the most opportunity for growth?

CHAPTER 2

Leaders Are Relational

The first thing great teachers do is get to know their students and build authentic relationships. Students know if teachers *genuinely* care about them or if caring seems to be just part of the job. Authenticity is difficult to fake. Building these real connections takes intentional investment: asking questions about students, listening, and finding ways to connect to their interests. Great teachers work hard in the early days of each school year to establish authentic relationships with each student. These trusted relationships build the foundation for deeper connection and engagement in the classroom. Researcher Ashley Peterson-DeLuca (2016) writes, "The research literature agrees: teachers need to be able to build trusting relationships with students in order to create a safe, positive and productive learning environment."

Leaders at each level should strive to build those relationships as well. This is another opportunity for building and district leaders to learn from teachers. People of all ages work harder for people who show genuine interest and concern for their well-being. By establishing relationships, leaders at every level will have that foundation of trust to build upon. Mike Kneebone, director of technology and media services at MSD Washington Township, shares a story about his move from the classroom into a district leadership role:

> When I first took over the department, it was divided, and many members of the team were disenfranchised. I believe that the source of it was [that] it didn't matter how hard you worked or didn't work, and talents weren't valued or leveraged. The organization was flat, and there wasn't a path of progression or growth. We had members of the team that had been allowed to skate by with doing very little. This drove home the perception that working hard at your job, having passion for it, and improving your knowledge and skill set were not valued. In fact, some felt punished by being assigned more work while others were paid the same, or in some cases more, for less work, knowledge, and skill.

The first thing I did as the leader of this team was take the personnel audit I was given and address the inequities it revealed. I met with each employee in a casual setting. The focus was learning about their life outside of work. What was their background? What were their hobbies and interests? Did they have family? How did they come to work for Washington Township? I shared the same information about myself to establish an understanding, a relationship beyond boss–employee.

Part of that meeting was also to hear their aspirations, interests, and goals. I committed to making them feel heard through my actions. I restructured the department from a flat organization with all twenty-eight people reporting to me, to a five-tiered organization based on skill set and responsibility. Where there was a good fit, I reassigned people to a position aligned to their skills and goals. I provided training for all staff. With a restructure of the department, I made funds available to incentivize professional learning through certification stipends. The other key was to commit to promoting from within. They needed to see that I was invested in them and that working hard, developing their knowledge, and staying in Washington Township paid off.

With the team feeling better about everyone pulling their weight and everyone getting their fair due, we needed to be galvanized to really bond them together. I'd compare it to bootcamp or pledging in college. There was not a lack of challenges or shortage of pain points impacting teachers and student learning. I simply had to pick one to rally around. I gave them clear scope and strategies to address it. They felt the autonomy to do what it took to fix the issue. The important part for me was to make sure they felt my support. When things didn't go well or work out, I took the blame and backlash as the "shield" for the department. When there were accolades to be had, I made sure that they were all theirs, and they were seen as the heroes. They began to feel safe trying new solutions and taking risks because they knew I had their backs.

As a team, we adopted a work hard, play hard mentality. We were brought together by overcoming challenges in the workplace. I organized regular social outings so everyone could learn more about one another beyond the workplace. When you care about those you work with and feel personally invested in everyone's well-being, you will work harder to protect the team. (M. Kneebone, personal communication, September 8, 2020)

Kneebone highlights several ways he forged relationships when he first moved into his current leadership role. The common themes that stand out are those of effective communication, positive mindset, and a healthy culture.

- **Effective communication:** He quickly established two-way communication when he met one on one with each employee at the beginning of his tenure in that role.

- **Positive mindset:** He fostered a growth mindset among the entire department by identifying common challenges and rallying around them as a team to produce solutions.

- **Healthy culture:** The culture shift was made when he restructured the flat organization into a five-tiered structure that promoted a more democratic style of leadership, giving each employee a voice.

All these developments were built on authentic relationships. Let's dig into each area.

Effective Communication

Educational leader Eric Sheninger (2016) notes that effective communication tactics "lay out all the pertinent details that address the what, why, and where while mitigating the small group of underminers present in any organization, school, or classroom" (p. 16). Communication goes well beyond what is being said and heard. Effective communication also requires active listening, including attending to nonverbal cues, consistent messaging across a variety of communication methods, and understanding the importance of communication to successful collaboration.

Listen Actively

If you are in a leadership position (and teachers, you are *all* the leaders of your classrooms, so this applies to you), do you take the time to actively process all that people are (and aren't) saying to you? The Center for Creative Leadership (2021) defines active listening like this: "a valuable technique that requires the listener to thoroughly absorb, understand, respond, and retain what's being said." Listening to understand is identified as a key leadership skill by Edward L. Baker, Abigail Dunne-Moses, Allan J. Calarco, and Roderick Gilkey (2019) in the *Journal of Public Health Management and Practice*. They add, "The most important benefits of effective listening are *relationship building* and the *enhancement of trust*" (Baker et al., 2019).

As good active listeners, strong leaders take in all the information available to them when they listen. They focus on body language, tone of voice, and the actual words they are hearing. Then, they start asking questions. This opens the door for the conversation to be directed by those they lead and not by the leader. These conversations often turn into impromptu coaching sessions. The communication shouldn't stop there. Leaders can maintain contact via email, short conversations in the hallway, and quick drop-ins with the only intention being to check on that teacher's well-being.

Let's look at how one teacher uses active listening strategies to build relationships with her students.

A Look at Leadership in a Classroom

Erin often refers to herself as her students' "school mom." She credits active listening as the catalyst to the relationships she builds with each student. She works hard to show how much she cares about them by listening and empathizing. She supports them both emotionally and academically, and those relationships last long past the students' final days in her classroom.

Erin shows us how caring about students' emotional well-being by listening to them builds the relationships necessary for her to get higher engagement in their academic lives. Ask some questions, and then listen to see how you can serve your students better.

We've already discussed the importance of building relationships, and those don't happen without a high level of trust. That trust is gained and fostered through active listening. Peter Miller (2012), professor at Southern Cross University, writes in *Today's Manager*:

> Genuinely listening to others requires intellectual and physical effort. . . . Active listening is listening for the full meaning of what is being transmitted and observing. It includes "listening" to the non-verbal clues contained with the message without making premature judgments or interpretations.

To be servant leaders, it's necessary to first be active listeners. Active listening makes the journey about those whom leaders are serving, and not just about a leadership title or position. So, ask questions, and then just listen.

Communicate Using a Variety of Methods

Good communication is key to building relationships and empowering students, teachers, and administrators (Hereford, n.d.). Methods of communication have changed much from when I entered the field of education in 1998. As the leader of my classroom, I communicated with parents through a parent night at the beginning of the year, parent–teacher conferences in the fall, and weekly newsletters. My building principal's communication methods were similar. I used those tools mostly to tell parents what we were working on in class and what would be coming in the near future.

Currently, however, leaders have a higher demand for regular and varied communication. Every piece of communication is a piece of the story the leader is trying to tell about the organization. It's an opportunity to be boring, or it's a chance to be inviting and engaging. Leaders can establish multiple pathways for communication that build on laying the foundations through relationships. Some easy ways include being visible at extracurricular events, chatting to families, and being open and welcoming out in the community. Leaders at every level can invite communication by having an open-door policy for stakeholders who want to engage face to face. Keep in mind that *open door* doesn't mean *any time*. Feel free to establish something akin to office hours to make it more conducive to your other responsibilities. Using video conferencing platforms such as Google Meet, Teams, and Zoom have made communicating even simpler for all involved. Many principals have also had success forming student advisory committees with students from various demographics to create more open pathways for communication.

Most of the stakeholders will be interacting regularly on social media, so leaders need to take daily communication to those platforms. If we want students and staff to use a variety of communication methods and digital tools, then the leaders must model doing so. Some examples include class or school Instagram accounts where students and teachers can post pictures of projects and events in real time. Facebook continues to be a favorite platform for many parents, so it becomes a great conduit for communicating about classroom, school, and district happenings. Athletic directors can tweet game results on Twitter. Products like ClassDojo (https://classdojo.com) and Remind (www.remind.com) make it simple for teachers to update parents without giving out personal cellphone numbers. Seesaw (https://web.seesaw.me) is a fantastic digital portfolio platform that makes it easy to invite parents to see their children's online activity as it happens. When it becomes part of the day, it takes only a few seconds to keep that line open between home and school, making everyone feel more connected.

Communicate to Collaborate

Ways of communicating are only one piece of the puzzle. Strong communication skills are essential for healthy collaboration. People aren't actually collaborating if they aren't steadily communicating about the goals they are trying to accomplish and outcomes they achieve. Effective collaboration is vital to successful practices regardless of industry.

Leaders in every industry are seeing the importance that strong communication and effective collaboration skills play in the success of an organization. Leaders are tasked with modeling (and sometimes teaching) best practices, as well as providing opportunities for application. Not every meeting needs to be collaborative, but an environment that promotes collaboration can also stimulate innovation. It's up to the leaders to build relationships that encourage the team mindset necessary for true collaboration to take place.

Digital communication tools also offer collaborative opportunities, allowing people to work simultaneously, or not, depending on the project and personal time constraints. It also allows meetings to take place in offices, airports, homes, and coffee shops. Technology plays an increasingly important role in how educators collaborate and often produces better, more thorough results. Leaders have the systems in place to aid communication and collaboration, but they must have other important aspects secured to produce efficient and effective results.

Paul Petrone (2019), head of Academic and Government Marketing for LinkedIn Learning, referenced the importance of collaboration in his blog post, "Why Collaboration Breaks Down—And How to Avoid It." The study found that collaboration breaks down when there is a lack of trust. If you don't trust the members of the team, then you tend to micromanage each component of the process and project. Leaders need to have a team composed of people who bring different skills to the table and who they trust to do their jobs in the group.

Collaboration also breaks down when one person is too attached to one idea. Leaders must have a growth mindset and be willing to hear each person's thoughts even if it differs from their own. A collaborative project needs to begin with a clear end goal. It's the leader's job to provide the clarity for that goal and the desired outcomes, and then show how these relate to the overall vision for the organization. Each team needs to establish group norms at the forefront of the project to keep everyone focused on individual accountability while working toward group responsibility. Everyone can keep the momentum moving when the norms and processes are clear and in place.

Positive Mindset

Carol Dweck (2016) is the foremost authority on the positive or growth mindset. In "What Having a 'Growth Mindset' Actually Means," she summarizes a growth mindset: "Individuals who believe their talents can be developed (through hard work, good strategies, and input from others) have a growth mindset" (Dweck, 2016). Active listening and effective communication are important ways to build relationships, and fostering a growth mindset is just as vital. While it is essential for teachers to encourage a growth mindset in their students, it's just as essential for leaders to nurture the same mindset in their teams.

Just like students in a classroom, adults have some specific needs when it comes to enhancing these shifts in mindset. If you are a leader, it's one of your responsibilities to provide them with, at least, these three requirements for enhancing a growth mindset: (1) clear, simple, direct objectives with some structure *and* freedom; (2) support, trust, and motivation; and (3) challenges.

Provide Clear, Simple, Direct Objectives With Some Structure and Freedom

I'm a huge proponent of student-driven learning. A common misconception of student-driven learning, however, is that it is unstructured. Truly effective student-driven learning has quite a bit of structure. It may be in the background, but it's there, guiding the learning. Similarly, a positive mindset will thrive when an individual has a clear objective to meet a certain outcome. A positive mindset requires structured thinking, in addition to freedom, to create and innovate in ways that call to a specific person. For this reason, I am a big fan of using choice boards, or learning menus, in the classroom. Choice boards are basically graphic organizers that allow students to choose from a variety of methods to direct and demonstrate their learning. Students are all learning the same material, but they may pick articles to read or videos to watch. They may decide to construct a 3-D model or create a multimedia presentation. They have many choices, giving them the freedom to choose the learning path most interesting to them. Students know the expectations from the beginning and then get to direct their learning. Leaders need to give that direction and structure and then get out of the way so students can create in freedom. Choice boards work well digitally, distributed through a learning management system, or they can be printed out as a paper graphic organizer of sorts. Choice boards aren't just for the classroom; they can make faculty meetings more engaging as well. Figures 2.1 and 2.2 (page 22) show examples.

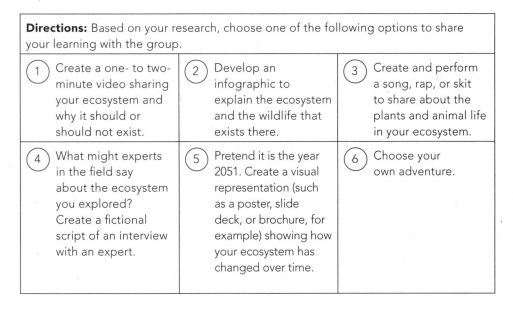

Directions: Based on your research, choose one of the following options to share your learning with the group.

(1) Create a one- to two-minute video sharing your ecosystem and why it should or should not exist.	(2) Develop an infographic to explain the ecosystem and the wildlife that exists there.	(3) Create and perform a song, rap, or skit to share about the plants and animal life in your ecosystem.
(4) What might experts in the field say about the ecosystem you explored? Create a fictional script of an interview with an expert.	(5) Pretend it is the year 2051. Create a visual representation (such as a poster, slide deck, or brochure, for example) showing how your ecosystem has changed over time.	(6) Choose your own adventure.

Figure 2.1: Classroom choice board.

Visit go.SolutionTree.com/leadership for a free reproducible version of this figure.

Directions: Choose one of the following options to support your own professional growth and share your learning with the group.

(1) Read a blog post or listen to a podcast and create a one- to two-minute video sharing how it will impact your work.	(2) Read a chapter of a professional book and develop an infographic to explain the key takeaways.	(3) Participate in an education Twitter chat and sketch your reflections of the conversation.
(4) Interview three to five students to discover what they like best about your class. Use that information to develop a lesson plan for the coming weeks.	(5) Read an article. Create a visual representation (such as a poster, slide deck, or brochure, for example) showing how you will apply the new learning to your work.	(6) Choose your own adventure.

Figure 2.2: Professional development choice board.

Visit **go.SolutionTree.com/leadership** for a free reproducible version of this figure.

Initiatives, both large and small, require communication that has clear direction for success. Let's look at how one superintendent provided the objectives and support for one of his team members to lead a 1:1 implementation.

A Look at Leadership in a District

Jay saw the need to provide leadership for adding technology throughout his district. Since his technology director did not come from an education background, he asked his curriculum director to spearhead a 1:1 steering committee. His objectives included ensuring all stakeholders were represented on the committee and using that school year to research and plan. The objectives were clear enough for the curriculum director to get started but also gave her the freedom to shape the work as it went. The steering committee visited schools that already had 1:1 implemented, attended conferences, and mapped out a clear plan for moving the initiative forward the following year. The superintendent met with the curriculum director regularly for updates but continued to let her drive the work. The clear objectives and continued conversations gave her the support she needed to face the challenge and determine the best path forward for the district.

Give Support, Trust, and Motivation

Have you heard of Genius Hour, 20 percent time, or passion projects? These ideas center on encouraging employees to put a portion of their time into projects that have meaning for them. As its name suggests, Google's 20 percent rule allows its employees to spend one full day each week on a project of personal interest. The company's founders, Larry Page and Sergey Brin (2004), wrote in their company IPO letter, "We encourage our employees, in addition to their regular projects, to spend 20% of their time working on what they think will most benefit Google. This empowers them to be more creative and innovative." It's the support and trust they receive from the leaders, along with the passion and excitement they have from pursuing something of their own, that lead to higher creative and innovative energy. These projects aren't just for Google and the elementary classroom. What if every leader had their own passion project? What if they encouraged every employee to pursue a passion project?

Imagine feeling trusted to lead your own growth through a passion project. Many school and district leaders have established cultures where little direction is necessary. Others might still be nurturing that healthy culture and need to provide a bit more support. The professional development choice board in figure 2.2 could be just the resource to guide an educator's first passion project. The key here is the trust leaders are placing in their team members. By encouraging personalized professional learning, they are fostering the growth mindset that healthy organizations embody. If you are a school or district leader unsure of how to lead a passion project endeavor, find teachers who are doing it in the classroom and go observe the process. Remember, leaders can learn from each other regardless of position.

Trust can and should be established and nurtured in multiple ways. Genuinely caring about the people you serve is the foundation of trust. Taking time to talk to people, ask them questions, and give them freedom to work and grow shows that you understand and trust them.

This culture of trust also extends to the encouragement and motivation of teams. The leaders of any successful organization know how important this is. Tim Stobierski (2019), contributing writer for Northeastern University, says, "Positive feedback helps your employees feel valued in their roles. When someone feels valued, they are more motivated to continue performing at their highest levels." The foundation of trust and growth that effective leaders can build allows people to be comfortable being vulnerable and taking risks. When team members know their leaders trust them to take risks, they look to those leaders for encouragement but not for them to solve the problem. This can only happen when the leader models these characteristics and leads by example.

Offer Challenges

New challenges, when introduced in a supportive environment, often breed a growth mindset. Without them, work can become stagnant. There is also a reciprocal relationship involved. As Dweck (2015) puts it, "The growth-mindset approach helps children feel good in the short *and* long terms, by helping them thrive on challenges and setbacks on their way to learning." These challenges lead to learning, growth, reflection, and creation. They stretch thinking and usually necessitate innovative thinking. Where some thrive with this kind of challenge, not everyone does. That is where the leader must find the right creative minds to pair with the right challenges.

For example, in the classroom, a teacher might institute a challenge corner. This could take many forms: everything from a puzzle on a table to a question posted in the classroom (or digitally) about a local issue that has arisen. Teachers challenge students to brainstorm around solving the challenge independently or with others. Inquiry-based learning and project-based learning frameworks naturally patch into challenging thinking. These types of projects encourage students to become problem identifiers as well as problem solvers.

Similarly, school and district leaders can use a design-thinking cycle during meetings to think through solutions to various school, district, or community challenges. The key is that no idea is off the table. This fosters a growth mindset and also nurtures trust and risk taking.

Healthy Culture

Jared T. Clark (2019), school leader, shared his research in the paper, "The Impact of School Culture upon an Educational Institution." He says, "In essence, culture is the way an organization thinks and acts. Culture is also defined as the framework that a group can use to solve problems" (Clark, 2019). In a healthy culture, people feel encouraged to try new things, take risks, and share their ideas. A collaborative spirit exists in which everyone is working for the benefit of the whole. Toxic cultures repress that freedom. The staff tends to be stressed, unhappy, or operating in silos—or even all three. When leaders build and foster a healthy culture, it plays an integral role in empowering people at all levels of the organization. Taking time to build real relationships and fostering a positive mindset are two ways to build a healthy culture. The best leaders all tend to share similar characteristics. They are servant leaders who cultivate a culture of trust and empower their teams to grow and thrive.

A healthy culture is one of the largest components of employee retention. Writer Matt D'Angelo (2018) shares thoughts from Heidi Mausbach, CEO of a digital marketing agency, in his article, "Build a Culture That Increases Employee Retention." He writes, "Mausbach said that building a better business culture is key to keeping employees engaged. . . . A Gallup study found that employees who are engaged at work are 59 percent less likely to look for a different job" (D'Angelo, 2018). That culture needs to be seen and heard by employees—and leaders, starting with the top district leaders, must model it. Staff members will know if the perceived culture is real or just for looks. When that healthy culture is envisioned, developed, and communicated, it more easily permeates at every level. There are specific ways a leader can build a healthy school culture: conduct a culture audit, involve stakeholders in decision making, make the culture visible, build community among staff members, and choose teams wisely while fostering collaboration.

Conduct a Culture Audit

A school culture audit consists of a survey of questions about the beliefs and assumptions of those in the school or district. The audit can also address existing activities and routines to give a broader picture of current culture. By giving stakeholders a survey, the leader can find strengths and potential weaknesses. The survey might ask questions or provide prompts such as "When something is not working in our school, the faculty and staff predict and prevent rather than react and repair" or "The school staff is empowered to make instructional decisions rather than waiting for supervisors to tell them what to do" (Wagner, 2006). Stakeholders can assign a score to each prompt, allowing leaders a way to view school culture in quantifiable terms. This will aid in prioritizing needs and finding the right place to begin.

At times, leaders can gather information informally; other times, a needs assessment is the best place to start. Not only will an audit give leaders pertinent information, but it increases employee engagement by giving them a voice. One that I've found particularly useful is in educational administration professor Christopher R. Wagner's (2006) article "The School Leader's Tool for Assessing and Improving School Culture" (https://bit.ly/3Ba4ACf). A culture audit is beneficial for all schools and districts, even those that aren't experiencing acute issues. Just as we want individuals to have a growth mindset, culture surveys help school and district leaders have a growth mindset when it comes to the health of the culture of the organization.

Involve Stakeholders in Decision Making

A study published by the Quaglia Institute for Student Aspirations and the Teacher Voice and Aspirations International Center (2014) finds a direct correlation between teacher voice and the culture of school. Anne O'Brien (2016) writes of the findings in *Edutopia*, "Teachers who are comfortable expressing honest opinions and concerns are four times more likely to be excited about their future career in education." If teachers and staff feel like they have a voice in the school's happenings, they will trust their leaders more, work harder for the benefit of the team, and take more ownership in development. Involving them in the processes and procedures of daily operations shows them that they are a valued and necessary part of the district.

Look at how elementary school principal Jeff tapped into teacher voice to drive a schoolwide change initiative. The impact went beyond the special education population it was intended for and benefited many students as a result.

A Look at Leadership in a School

When Jeff became principal, he started to realize a problem with the special education program. Students with IEPs were being pulled out of the general education classroom multiple times a day. The students felt marginalized, and the stigma created for them was very real. He brought the issue to his leadership team, which comprised teachers from each grade level. He got their input and their ideas on how to solve the problem. Two teachers championed a push-in model to get things moving. Those teachers' grade levels piloted the idea, and although it was messy, the positive effects were quickly apparent. Students were more immersed in the overall school culture, and teachers noticed improvements in their self-esteem. On top of that, other students, not identified as having special needs, benefited from having the special education teachers in their classrooms. Often these teachers and paraprofessionals are able (and willing) to assist other students who are sitting nearby who may need help. Having someone who is specifically trained to help students with special needs also frees up the general education teacher to help others. Jeff knows that if this had been a top-down implementation driven by him, the buy-in or ownership of the change that came from peers leading the movement would have been missing. With teachers' voices leading the cause, it caught on faster.

Jeff saw a need to better serve students with special needs in his school. By taking the problem to a group of teacher leaders, he was able to get their input and make their voices heard. His democratic approach to leadership created more ownership among the staff and realized higher returns for the students.

Make the Culture Visible

In any school district, leaders need to clearly understand, consistently communicate, and model the district's mission, vision, values, and goals. When all stakeholders are aware of these foundational values, they have greater insight into the culture and embrace it. Leaders can communicate these values in a variety of ways, from social media posts to physical posters within the workspace. Portia Newman (2019), education leader and consultant, says, "Leadership should identify clear expectations about the school environment. . . . Expectations should be clear for students and staff. . . .

These clear expectations keep everyone aligned to the overall mission and vision of the school." When employees understand the mission and values of the organization and when they enjoy where they work, they will help make that culture more visible through their own communications with others.

Figure 2.3 (page 28) will help you and your team develop a shared mission, vision, values, and goals.

Build Community Among Staff Members

One way to build community within the school among staff members is by holding social gatherings outside of the workday. These could be for mini-celebrations, holidays, or strictly for the sake of socializing. Staff will be more willing to take risks and more willing to work together if they care about one another as people first. People can also connect using virtual community-building options and video platforms. Just like the in-person ideas, these can be strictly for socializing, or leaders can organize them by topics of interest or problems of practice. Several people could volunteer to host a virtual room (or in person) around a topic of interest. These could be education related or just for fun. Similarly, individuals could come with a common problem of practice (such as students not engaging in online work, lack of communication with parents, and so on) and host a room to gather ideas and possible solutions from colleagues. All of these ideas take little time to set up, but they go a long way in building community.

Choose Teams Wisely While Fostering Collaboration

It is the leader's responsibility to form teams and get people in the right places to utilize their talents and passions to better the organization. The best teams comprise people who bring different gifts and viewpoints to the table but share a common goal and mindset. Lisa B. Kwan (2019), writer for *Harvard Business Review*, says:

> Leaders understand the central role that cross-group collaboration plays in business today. It's how companies of all shapes and sizes . . . plan to innovate, stay relevant, and solve problems that seem unsolvable. . . . In short, it's how companies plan to succeed, compete, and just survive.

It all comes back to a positive work culture built on fostering relationships. The good news is that leaders can change cultures. They can build trust. They can discover and define visions. And they can teach effective communication and collaboration strategies. When everyone is invested in the culture, everyone benefits. Each leader, regardless of position, has the responsibility to invest in the organization by investing in building relationships.

Describe each area (building, grade level, or department) of your school or district in the left-hand column and the current state of each topic for your entire organization in the right-hand column.	
Area 1:	Culture:
Area 2:	Teachers:
Area 3:	Parents:
Area 4:	Students:
Area 5:	Curriculum:
Area 6:	Financials:
Area 7:	Performance:
Area 8:	Media or brand:

Look for trends and identify the key organizational values.
•   •   •   •   •   •
Add your vision statement here.   The vision statement should encapsulate the core values and be future oriented. It will guide initiatives and keep all stakeholders focused.

Add your mission statement here. The mission statement shows all stakeholders why your organization exists and how it benefits all students.	
Use the following prompts to assist in goal setting. Read the prompts in the left-hand column, then fill in your goals in the right-hand column. Each prompt provides space for three goals, but feel free to construct less or more as to fit your vision and mission.	
Identify the initiative. • Why is it important?	
Connect to current initiatives. • How do they interrelate?	
Develop a shared vision. • Determine who it impacts and how you can include them in developing the shared vision.	
Identify the initiative. • Why is it important?	
Connect to current initiatives. • How do they interrelate?	
Develop a shared vision. • Determine who it impacts and how you can include them in developing the shared vision.	
Identify the initiative. • Why is it important?	
Connect to current initiatives. • How do they interrelate?	
Develop a shared vision. • Determine who it impacts and how you can include them in developing the shared vision.	

Figure 2.3: Mission, vision, values, and goals framework.

*Visit **go.SolutionTree.com/leadership** for a free reproducible version of this figure.*

Table 2.1 shares ways leaders build relationships at the classroom, school, and district levels.

Table 2.1: Leadership at a Glance—Lessons for Building Relationships

Focus Point	Leadership in a Classroom	Leadership in a School	Leadership in a District
Effective Communication	Find chances to learn about your students. • Talk to them as they come into the classroom or other times you see them in the hallways. • Design lessons that show insights into their personalities and interests. • Make sure you spend time listening to them. • Use newsletters, phone calls, emails, and texts as important ways of communicating with homes.	Find chances to learn about the faculty and staff in your school. • Meet with them one on one where they get to talk about their personal lives and you share about yours. • Have an open-door policy where people feel comfortable stopping in. • Connect with staff outside of the school building as often as possible. • Social media is a great way to communicate with homes on the great things happening in the school.	Find chances to learn about all stakeholders. • Be visible in classrooms, schools, and extracurricular events to open opportunities for conversation. • Consider a council with students that truly represent the entire body to stay connected with classrooms. • Consider a similar council comprising teachers. • Social media is the place to tell the district story. Communicate the goodness happening at all levels.

Growth Mindset	Openly discuss the differences between fixed and growth mindsets with your students. • Provide challenges that encourage them to think critically and work collaboratively. Value the progress more than the product. • The emphasis should always be on the learning and not the grade.	Model and promote growth mindsets to staff; these are important for all students, so it's extremely important for principals to do this with staff. • Identify building-level challenges together. • Brainstorm solutions. • Put them into practice.	Empower people on your teams so that district-level challenges don't fall on one person. • Set objectives. • Give clear direction. • Provide support as needed. • Get out of the way.
Healthy Culture	Build community from day one. • Have activities in place from the first day of school that allow each student to be recognized as a valuable part of the classroom.	Make time for social gatherings. • Celebrate successes. • Have fun together! Involve teachers and staff in decision making. • They are on the front lines and their voices matter.	Clearly define the mission, vision, values, and goals of the school district. • Communicate these with frequency and consistency. Conduct a culture audit. • All stakeholders need to be represented. • Act on the data you collect.

Questions for Growth and Reflection

The following questions offer an opportunity to reflect on this chapter's content and think about what you might be able to work on.

1. What are your main modes of communication? What messages do you communicate consistently?

2. How do you maintain a growth mindset in yourself? In what ways can you promote a growth mindset in those you lead?

3. How do you identify your risk takers? How are you encouraging people to rise to challenges? What challenges are you personally accepting for creation and innovation?

4. How would you currently identify the culture of your classroom, building, or district?

5. In what ways can you foster a healthier culture?

CHAPTER 3

Leaders Are Innovative

Every person is born with creative potential. In student-driven classrooms, students receive the opportunity, space, and encouragement to stretch and strengthen those potential creative muscles. In a time when educators are forced to focus on testing and standards, creativity and innovation often get pushed to the side. It doesn't have to be this way. It may require some extra thinking and planning, but increasing creative and innovative thinking can, and should be, a part of any rich, standards-based curriculum. Digital education expert Justin Raudys (2020) points out, "As most educators know, the traditional, teacher-focused, lecture-style teaching method can lead to disengagement and boredom (for both teachers and students) quite quickly." He goes on to identify innovative teaching strategies including using project-based learning, inquiry-based learning, experiential learning activities, and differentiated instruction, among others.

Likewise, building- and district-level leaders need to create environments where educators can flex those innovation muscles. Elementary principal and author Michael Earnshaw promotes innovation in both his teachers and his students. He shares his thoughts on how this is a responsibility of leaders at every level:

> Teachers today are continually being asked by their administrators two things: (1) Build relationships with your students, and (2) be innovative. These two items are key ingredients for any successful classroom. Any good teacher knows that if they want their students to succeed, to know their strengths and weaknesses, to be comfortable collaborating and problem solving with peers, and to leave our schools determined to change the world, that teacher must ensure a trusting relationship with their students and bring innovative approaches to their lessons.
>
> What about building administrators? Are the same expectations placed on them? The answer is, *somewhat*. Yes, principals and assistant principals are expected to know their staff and push their staff to bring rigor to their lessons. The problem with this antiquated approach is that it's not modeling what we expect from our teachers. How can I, as the instructional leader of our school, expect my

staff to create meaningful relationships when I am not modeling that expectation? How can I expect my staff to bring engaging, thought-provoking lessons to their students when I simply read bullets off a PowerPoint during a staff meeting? Without administrators walking the walk, our classrooms will never reach their potential destiny.

If you ever come to our school to visit or call my office to have a conversation, you're not going to find me. I've learned that for me to build meaningful, collaborative, and trusting relationships, I need to get out of the office and be with others. The school has become my office and I am with teachers and students all day, every day. You'll find me rolling down the halls on my skateboard, pushing a mobile desk. Sometimes I will stop at a busy intersection of hallways and work. I'm doing the same tasks every other principal is completing, but I'm with those that matter most. I'm visible, approachable, and am confidently able to say I know exactly what is happening in our school. I'm able to work with staff and teachers at a moment's notice, making everyone a little stronger.

I don't expect kids to sit at a desk, copying notes from a lecture, so I make sure to not do that with our staff during meetings. You may find us outside in a circle standing on Struggle Island, sharing issues we're facing, and helping each other get through them. Or staff will be "Speed Dating," seated across from each other, sharing their highlights of an article they read for three minutes, and then one row moves to the left to have a new conversation with a new "date." Or sometimes you just need to have some fun and paint pumpkins replicating your favorite children's book!

School leaders, get out of your offices, and stop reading information to your staff that could be sent in an email. If you want your staff to build relationships with their students and bring innovation to the classroom, you must do the same. Model what you expect, and I promise you will see worlds change. (M. Earnshaw, personal communication, October 23, 2020)

Glenn Llopis (2014), an expert on leadership strategy, writes, "Innovation requires a certain type of person: they are passionate explorers in pursuit of endless possibilities." Michael demonstrates that pursuit is open to anyone who wants to develop those innovation muscles: by building a culture of innovation and creating, cultivating, and sustaining creative environments. He shows us that while it is essential for teachers to foster a creative and innovative mindset in their students, it's just as essential for leaders to nurture the same mindset in their teams.

Culture of Innovation

Educational leader and president of a professional learning firm Amos shares how he uses innovative practices in the hiring process—something that would benefit school- and district-level leaders. Let's see what he does that may be different than traditional interviews.

A Look at Leadership in a District

In education and most other industries, the job interview serves the traditional purpose of seeking and selecting talent. As practical as this process might be, learning organizations and candidates often struggle to strike a sustainable, mutually rewarding fit.

Amos builds his team differently. He reserves approximately 10 percent of his leadership bandwidth to nurture a prospect pipeline through a sequence of open-ended, inquiry-based conversations with interested educators.

Initial conversations are unrushed visits that welcome educators to share details of their leadership journey as well as to share philosophies and career aspirations. Amos then aligns details of each educator's share with an overview of the firm's values and a brief snapshot of its history.

With this foundation in place, nascent relationships emerge. Over the course of four to six additional conversations scheduled over two to five months, Amos facilitates a process anchored by the following outcomes:

- Share and reflect on an artifact from the field (student work, curriculum sample, blog post or other media post). What insights does it reveal?

- Review two to three case studies that unpack how the organization operates. How does the educator envision supporting communities through this model?

- Follow a current employee in the field. What questions and epiphanies emerge?

- Co-facilitate one or more days. In what ways did this experience validate and challenge expectations?

- Pending a willingness to move forward, forge a partnership that enables successful first steps.

This approach has enabled Amos to attract, align, place—and most importantly, retain—talented, values-aligned education leaders. This process has guided the firm's growth from three to sixty-five members through at least three substantial spikes in growth.

While most district leaders don't have several months to vet potential employees, the practices Amos implements are replicable in districts and schools. Are you hinging the success of your teams and your organization on an application and a couple of interviews? Or are you taking time to really get to know candidates and to ensure that philosophies of education and values align with the school district? Districts need to replicate that culture of innovation. Classroom leaders can take a similar approach when forming collaborative groups. When teachers really know their students, they can help them form teams to do their best work.

Implementing new initiatives is always an opportunity to practice innovative thinking. I've worked with many school districts that have implemented a 1:1 technology initiative. They have experienced a variation in success. The success of an implementation isn't based on the device, the grade levels, or the learning management system. It all centers on the leadership and the existing culture. Were all of the leaders part of the vision surrounding the implementation? Are all of the leaders good at communicating the expectations clearly and positively to their teachers? Even if they disagree with certain components behind closed doors, leaders need to present a united front to the school's staff, parents, and students. Are they receiving good and ongoing professional learning opportunities ahead of the teachers?

Ben, a principal, is a great example of how thinking innovatively about a new initiative brought about a schoolwide transformation in how teaching and learning looked in the classroom. He always wanted the best for his students and staff. While he expected a lot, he in turn offered support, resources, and an open mind.

A Look at Leadership in a School

Ben volunteered his school to be one of six pilot schools for a technology implementation initiative. It would involve two of his teachers and one instructional coach working with a coach from Advanced Learning Partnerships, a professional development firm. These educators had one-on-one job-embedded coaching rounds throughout the school year to learn how to authentically integrate technology into everyday teaching and learning. When Ben saw how successful the pilot was, he wanted to implement it for all of his teachers. He approached the district director of instructional technology with an idea to bring the coach back the following year to work with his entire staff during their grade-level collaborative team meetings. Ben's idea sparked a new endeavor with Advanced Learning Partnerships and scaled student-driven learning practices to his entire school in less than one school year.

Ben's innovative thinking benefited his entire staff, and in turn, the entire student body. He had an idea that was different from the proposed model for the district, and he had the support from his leaders to implement it. Because Ben had already built a culture of innovation in his building, he had buy-in from the teachers as well.

But what are some specific ways to encourage this type of innovative thinking among all stakeholders? I can recommend two: (1) rethink staff meetings and (2) nurture organizational warmth.

Rethink Staff Meetings

We've all sat in those meetings wondering, for example, why on earth we are still debating what color to paint the staff restroom. If it's not that exact debate, it's something equally inconsequential in the lives of students and staff. I remember going to monthly whole-staff meetings as a classroom teacher. They would usually begin with housekeeping items, then sometimes there would be an article to read and discuss. Other times there would be data to analyze. But at the end of the meeting, we never really did anything with that information. I don't remember ever leaving a single one feeling energized or like what I just did was worthwhile. And I taught for fourteen years. That's a lot of time that I could've spent in better ways.

As a district administrator, the meetings were more frequent and much longer in duration. The difference was that they were conducted around a conference table, and we had the agenda about a week prior to the meeting in a Google Doc that we could add to. Although there were still times that I felt disconnected, most of these meetings were more purposeful. Since each administrator had an equal voice at the table, we were more involved in the process.

Now, as a full-time consultant, my meetings look vastly different. The majority of my work occurs with educators from states all over the country. Our meetings are conducted by phone, video conference, and sometimes just a shared Google Doc. These are the most streamlined and effective meetings I've ever been a part of. Which kind of meeting describes what you do in your school or district? How can you rethink staff meetings to be more innovative and become something people actually look forward to and benefit from? Let's look at these three key points.

1. **The power of the written word:** When possible, share any written information prior to the meeting. Share articles to read, data to review, policies to peruse or refine, and upcoming events via email and shared drives. You can use a learning management system to post resources, links, videos, and other instructional material. Pose discussion questions that the teachers can respond to and assignments for specific tasks the teachers need to complete and submit. Social media forums are also great platforms to encourage discussion and share articles and videos. I even know principals who have conducted entire staff meetings using hashtags on Twitter. It's a great way to expose teachers to this forum.

2. **The power of video conferencing:** Not all meetings have to be face to face. Likely, everyone got all too familiar with this concept throughout the

COVID-19 pandemic. This was a necessary innovation that arose from need and can easily transfer back into the workplace. Save time driving all over the district by holding the meetings via Google Hangouts, Skype, Zoom, Adobe Connect . . . you get the idea. These are especially nice for administrator meetings, committee meetings that are districtwide, initial interviews with potential employees, and of course, meeting with peers who are not local.

3. **The power of video recording:** Recording a message that isn't intended to be interactive is a great way to disseminate announcements, directions on how to do something new, or go over handbook policies. Apps like Screencastify (www.screencastify.com) are perfect for this and have an extremely low learning curve. It's easy to use and works on any computer.

   a. Plan your vision for the meeting.

   b. Create a Google Slides presentation with the information you would cover during a meeting.

   c. Use Screencastify to record your presentation.

   d. Upload the recording to Google Drive or YouTube or share directly on Google Classroom (or your compatible learning management system).

   e. Share the video with your staff prior to (or in place of) a face-to-face meeting.

By flipping your staff meetings, the actual face-to-face time becomes a much more authentic use of that time together. I'm a big believer in modeling what you expect to see in the classroom. If you are working to personalize instruction for your students, then you need to personalize learning for the teachers as well. Planning for more efficient use of that meeting time allows for this to take shape. Meeting time can become Genius Hour for Teachers.

Figure 3.1 is a personal passion project framework to use to frame your learning.

To foster creativity and this authentic use of meeting time, leaders need to empower teachers to drive their own learning. Show them how to build and tap into global networks of learning through Twitter, Facebook, LinkedIn, Pinterest, and blogs. These are valuable resources that can help them with that anytime, anywhere type of learning you want to nurture.

The leaders set the tone for this type of culture of innovation. They need to model innovative thinking, learning, and practice in their everyday lives and in how they conduct regular business in the classroom, school, and district. They need to be effective communicators with their teachers and a cheerleader for change. Why not start with rethinking staff meetings?

Topic

How will this project help you grow as an educator and leader?

What is your project title?

Briefly describe your project idea.

Will you produce a product? If so, what will it be?

Background Knowledge:

What do you already know about your topic?

What resources will I need to help me achieve my goal? (Record people, tools, media, and so on)

What experiences might I need in order to develop new understanding and skills?

Time Line

How many hours do you anticipate needing for your project? What milestones or benchmarks can you establish to guide your progress? How can you break these into daily or weekly activities?

Date	Milestone

Figure 3.1: Personal passion project.

continued ▶

Roadblocks	
Identify possible challenges you may encounter and some solutions that could help you move past them.	
Roadblock	Solution
Roadblock	Solution
Roadblock	Solution
Audience	
Upon completion, who will you share your project with? Does it benefit any stakeholders outside of yourself?	

*Visit **go.SolutionTree.com/leadership** for a free reproducible version of this figure.*

Nurture Organizational Warmth

Leaders also need to know what to look for when they walk into the classrooms in their schools. Successful innovation begins and ends with the culture of the organization. Are the leaders relational? Do they seek insight from those they serve? The culture needs to be one of positivity and mutual respect, one that opens the door for learning through failure. I call this organizational warmth.

Just like the leaders of the classroom need to create an environment where students are willing to take risks, the building and district leaders need to make sure their employees feel comfortable trying new things without fear of repercussion if it fails the first time. Leaders should inspire and motivate through modeling. If teachers and students are expected to be open to change and innovation, then the leaders should be modeling change and innovative mindsets through their own practices. Are some staff meetings held virtually? Are newsletters delivered digitally? Are leaders involved in ongoing professional learning? For example, if students are to be utilizing Google Drive, then the teachers, principals, and district administrators should be using that suite of applications as well.

In any organization, a successful and sustainable culture of creativity and innovation requires organizational warmth, leaders who model expected practices and mindsets, and clear communication at every level. Social psychologist, author, and educator Devon Price (2019) highlights the need for organizational warmth in creating that culture of innovation. In his article, "Innovation and Organizational Culture: How to Foster Innovative Thinking and Promote Innovation in an Organization," Price (2019) writes:

> As member of an organization, regardless of manager or employee, you must take responsibility for influencing your organization's culture, to create a workplace that is both comfortable and challenging, in which everyone is free to produce big ideas that may, sometimes, fail.

Author, speaker, and leadership strategist Michelle M. Smith (2015) wrote an article titled, "6 Ways the Best Leaders Innovate and Bring Great Ideas to Life." She points out, "Research shows 52 percent of employees are frustrated at work because leaders don't support their ideas or empower their creativity" (Smith, 2015). The article was more about generating and growing ideas in the workplace, yet most of it could be applied to leadership development. How can you cultivate innovation in yourself and your teams?

Author Todd Henry (2018) echoes that sentiment in his book, *Herding Tigers*. He says, "Leading is about more than just hitting your objectives; it's about helping your team discover, develop, and unleash its unique form of brilliance" (Henry, 2018, p. 6).

Holly is a veteran high school English teacher. Her passion for education has only grown throughout her career, but so has her awareness of "playing the game" of school. Read about how district mandates are squashing the opportunities for authentic teaching in her classroom.

A Look at Leadership in a Classroom

Holly took part in a professional development workshop centered around student engagement. One strategy mentioned was using choice boards to encourage more student autonomy and creativity. Her colleague, Phil, immediately spoke up when shown an example of a choice board containing nine different boxes. He asked if there were nine different objectives being learned on that choice board and how to justify the use of it if an administrator showed up in the room that day. Holly agreed. She said that over the years, the mandate to post the objectives being taught and the insistence that they do not deviate from that during the lesson had caused stress in the teachers and a shift from using authentic teaching methods back to lecturing so that they would not come under fire from their building leader.

That measure of accountability is causing students to miss opportunities to explore innovation and foster creative thinking skills. Teachers like Holly are still finding ways to integrate best practices while meeting the demands of their administrators, but they are doing it with one hand tied behind their backs. Holly regularly uses choice boards so that students get choices on how they learn and how they demonstrate their learning. By offering these choices, she gives them various creative outlets beyond the traditional test or essay to show growth. Holly would love to implement project-based learning and Genius Hour but is unsure of how to make sure her students are learning the posted objectives that day. That's where the culture of innovation plays such a vital role. That culture, built at the district level and perpetuated at the building and classroom levels, ensures that students learn the content while enabling them and their teachers to be creative in the process.

Cultivate and Sustain Creative Environments

Taylor Cone (2019), leadership coach, writes, "What separates good innovation leadership from great innovation leadership is the ability to create, cultivate, and sustain environments where everyone adds fuel to the collaborative fire."

The great part is that there are small steps you can take to create, cultivate, and sustain those creative environments to foster innovation in the classroom, building, and district.

1. **Own your fears, so they can't own you:** Change is inevitable in the world of education, but never so much so as in the 2019–2020 school year, when the COVID-19 pandemic forced radical alterations in education practice that are still unfolding. It has left educators everywhere overwhelmed, underfunded, and a bit fearful. They are expected to raise standardized test scores, integrate technology, adapt the curriculum to new standards, teach character education, make learning engaging, and remember to love the students.

    Most educators have probably heard that they can't keep doing something just because it's the way they've always done it. The problem is, fear of change often keeps them locked into the current routines. Take technology integration. A big fear is that the students will know more than the teachers about technology, so that the teacher's ability to lead the classroom might be undermined when one or more of their students prove more tech savvy. This scenario might be true, but it might not—and in any case, the student's tech savvy (or the teacher's lack of it) is not the issue. The issue is that the teacher fears loss of control in the classroom. But a teacher's leadership is based on more than just what a teacher knows that a student doesn't. Their students really might know more about how the technology works than the teachers do. And that's perfectly OK—the teachers can still guide how the students use that knowledge for growth. For example, those students can take on a leadership role in showing the teacher and other, less knowledgeable students how to do something. They will take more ownership in the classroom, and teachers will show that they value student-centered learning. When students see their teachers open to new ideas, they will be more open, as well. Open minds are the key component to innovative minds.

2. **Set goals to try something new on a regular basis:** If you just say that you will try something new, chances are it won't happen. Set short- and long-term goals, and don't be afraid to change them. Then, schedule a time to work toward that goal. Put it on your calendar and stick to it. Even if you only devote thirty minutes a week toward a goal, just do it. Any activity is better than no activity. This applies to the students in your classroom as well. Teach them why goal setting is vital to their learning, and then show them how to write effective goals. This would be a perfect place to introduce the Genius Hour concept. You can help them unleash their creativity in a Genius Hour project of their own. As leaders, by encouraging students and staff to set goals and try new things, you are also encouraging them to have a growth mindset, which, as pointed out, is key.

3. **Be a team player:** "Innovations are typically team efforts that are best led by passionate improvement co-champions" (Smith, 2015). I foster my own personal and professional learning by collaborating with other people. Twitter and LinkedIn are two of my favorite (and easiest) places to connect. I can ask questions, discuss ideas, and gain knowledge all while building a powerful network. Smith (2015) also encourages leaders to "reach across functional boundaries and tap into the talent of others." This works in the classroom as well when you allow students to collaborate and make passion-based learning a norm. The students will become more innovative through working with their peers. Thinking outside of the traditional classroom walls allows students to work with peers across the hall, across the district, or across the world. Technology definitely makes the world smaller and more collaborative.

4. **Intentionally facilitate learning to enhance creative thinking skills:** Most people can increase their level of creativity and innovative thinking. These aren't isolated skills that you can assess in your students on a standardized test. They are, however, the best skills you can nurture to help them be successful after high school. I have heard, "I'm just not creative," often from other adults. I think that is misguided thinking. We all contain the ability to be creative, we just need to find where that creativity takes root. Leon Ho (2018), speaker, writer, and entrepreneur, agrees. In his article, "What is Creativity? We All Have It, and Need It," he writes, "The fact is, that

everyone has an innate creative ability. Despite what most people may think, creativity is a skill that everyone can learn and hone on" (Ho, 2018). Again, this is where Genius Hour or passion projects come into play. Not only are learners driving their own learning, they're doing so in an area where they can allow their creative thinking skills to bloom. They get to be creative in *what* they learn, *how* they learn it, and how they *showcase* their learning.

5. **Smile:** I understand that this last one might sound a bit hokey—but stick with me. It really is part of creativity. Be open minded, take risks, embrace failure as progress, and have fun doing it. And if you can do all these things, you will smile as you become more innovative. Life is just better when you are having fun living it.

Creating something is immensely satisfying and empowering. Often, the paths to innovation are crooked and unclear. I've discovered the freedom in giving myself permission to travel those paths to the unknown. Let's makes those experiences possible for our students, teachers, and administrators as well. Empower learners of all ages and encourage them to free themselves from preconceived notions—to be risk takers. Through empowerment and freedom come true creativity. Just like good leaders never stop learning, they should never stop creating either.

Table 3.1 shares ways leaders can build and model a culture of innovation and cultivate and sustain creative environments.

Table 3.1: Leadership at a Glance—Strategies for Innovation

Focus Point	Leadership in a Classroom	Leadership in a School	Leadership in a District
Build a Culture of Innovation	Create a community where students know it's safe to take risks. Model for them how to learn and grow from failure. Put the emphasis on the learning and not the final product.	Find a way to showcase innovative work that teachers and students are doing.	Lay the foundation for a culture of innovation by being a team member who works alongside other educators and models a growth mindset.

Cultivate and Sustain Creative Environments	Allow students to collaborate on a passion-based learning project. This type of project-based learning is authentic, and the way students share their projects leads to higher levels of creativity. Provide time and space for your students to take part in Genius Hour projects. Setting up benchmarks along the way gives them the structure to keep learning on pace.	Set goals to regularly try something new and share it with your teachers and students, when appropriate. Make your learning process transparent. Rethink staff meetings to reserve time for teacher-driven Genius Hour projects.	Set goals to regularly try something new and share it with the other leaders in the district. Make your learning process transparent and model the risks you are willing to take to be innovative. Make creativity and innovation a district focus. Provide resources and opportunities for students and staff both to create.

Questions for Growth and Reflection

The following questions offer an opportunity to reflect on this chapter's content and think about what you might be able to work on.

1. What is a topic of interest that you are passionate about?
2. How do or can you set aside time to pursue that passion?
3. What do you do when you encounter failure?
4. What do you do when your students or employees experience failure?
5. What is a problem of practice you have experienced in your career that could use some innovative thinking to solve?

CHAPTER 4

Leaders Are Flexible

O ne of the very first lessons an educator learns is the importance of being flexible. You discover you'll have a new student suddenly joining your class. Or there is a convocation that has been called at the last minute. Or the school's internet server went down mid-morning, leaving you without many of your interactive teaching tools for that afternoon. There are endless surprises in the world of teaching. That same need to be open minded and adapt to whatever the day brings happens at every level of educational leadership—from the classroom to the school building to the district. Robert Dillon, a retired school and district administrator, shared one memory where being flexible was the best thing he could do for his teacher and for the students involved:

> "All ideas are good ideas" is something that you may hear in a brainstorm meeting or an aspirational comment from a keynote speaker, but allowing this to be your north star as a school leader can be extremely difficult. Even the most flexible of leaders can want to embrace ideas and potential solutions, but when they hear them for the first time, these "bad ideas" clash with the way you have done things, the way you understand research, the way the community will react, and most important, what the superintendent or board of education may think. Though my tenure as a school leader was rich in ideas, including the melding of ideas of students, teachers, parents, our community, and the solutions hatched in other districts, there were still moments when my flexibility was tested.
>
> "Let's have students climb in the tree."
>
> It seemed like a random, end-of-the-day, standing-at-bus-duty sort of comment from one of my science teachers. Just banter to fill up what was a noisy day for both of us. My initial thought was, *why in the world would we have students climb this one-hundred-foot oak tree in the middle of our parking lot?* Not a single branch started for thirty feet.

My reply was sarcastic: "Sounds awesome until someone falls to their death." Definitely not the most flexible tone and mindset that I could have brought to the conversation.

Thankfully, the science teacher was undeterred, and he started to unpack a plan that he had clearly spent some time developing. There were, apparently, certified tree climbers who could partner with our school to provide this tree climbing experience. They would provide the safety equipment and procedures. They would teach the physics of tree climbing and provide students with a unique perspective of the campus and the community.

This "bad idea" seemed like it was turning the corner into a possibility right here in the parking lot, but this shift from fixed to flexibility mindset was only possible because of a deep commitment to having a culture of *yes* in the DNA of the organization. We worked hard as a team to support and cultivate ideas, remain idea rich, and break through siloed thinking. Even with this mentality as a leader, it is hard to stay flexible in the exact moment that a "bad idea" is presented.

So, what happened with that "bad idea"? It turned out to be a *great* idea, and it continues today. Thousands of students have put on the safety harness, worked in teams, committed to the hard work of using the mechanical advantage to hoist themselves five stories or more off the ground, and returned to the classroom with a unique experience to bring their learning of physics to life.

The flexibility of leaders isn't a moment in time—if it were, I would have failed miserably—but is a pattern over time that stretches across every decision and every verbal and non-verbal reaction. It is the excitement that you have when new ideas emerge. It is the humility of saying that your doubts were wrong, and others had it right. It is the ability and flexibility to raise up the work of others and stand behind them as they are honored for their work. It is a journey as well. More experience allowed me to see the genius in others in new ways, and that new flexibility allowed me to serve in meaningful new ways. (R. Dillon, personal communication, September 13, 2020)

In sharing this story, Dillon showcases how having an open mind and being adaptive lead to success as a flexible leader. What if Dillon had just said no to the science teacher's idea about tree climbing? What type of leadership message would that send to his teachers? Keep in mind the importance of building relationships. If he had said no, without having an open mind, his students would have been robbed of an amazing educational experience, and it likely would have caused some damage in his relationship with that teacher as well. By being open minded, however, he showed flexibility in his thinking and willingness to adapt to do what was best for his students. In this chapter, we'll discuss how having an open mind and willingness to adapt are both key to flexible thinking, as well as how even making mistakes and experiencing failure can be immensely valuable.

An Open Mind

Christina Lattimer (2018), leadership coach and consultant, writes:

> Part of being open-minded is being able to see another's point of view and evaluating not whether it is right or wrong, but whether it works or not . . . . An open-minded leader will honour other people and the choices they make.

The Positive Psychology Center (2004) at the University of Pennsylvania, of which renowned psychologist and professor Martin Seligman is the director, highlights open-mindedness as a major strength. Research suggests that open-minded individuals are less likely to be swayed by single events and manipulation and can better predict how others will behave without projecting (Positive Psychology Center, 2004).

The *Houston Chronicle* (2021), in the midst of the COVID-19 pandemic, a time when open-mindedness when searching for solutions became more important than ever, points out, "Open-mindedness is critical to job success because some problems can't be solved using old techniques." Open-mindedness leads to higher flexibility and the ability to adapt, which in turn leads to greater opportunities, meaning teams whose members are open minded experience much more success. In education settings, one can see how that characteristic would lead to higher levels of communication and collaboration.

Open-minded leaders can take in the big picture. They participate in meetings at every level of educational leadership, from department meetings to school board meetings. Arguably, the most important item to bring to any meeting is an open mind. Many great ideas are ignored strictly due to someone not having an open mind about it. It's often easier to say no than to hear out a proposal, plan a process for success, and say yes to whatever is being asked. It's easier, but not better. Great leaders maintain an open mind. That doesn't mean they always say yes, but they listen and use discernment before making decisions. Some great ways to foster an open mindset include the following.

- Ask a lot of questions.
- Be an active listener.
- Don't be afraid to step outside of your comfort zone.
- Use processes (for example, decision trees) to think through various solutions.
- Postpone making a decision when more thought is required.

There are several methods that can assist leaders in making decisions. A framework such as a decision tree can help you organize your thoughts whether you're making a decision independently or as a team. There are digital flowcharts that you can create to think through it, or use a ready-made graphic organizer. Figure 4.1 provides a decision tree template. Educators at any level can utilize decision trees to guide their thought processes.

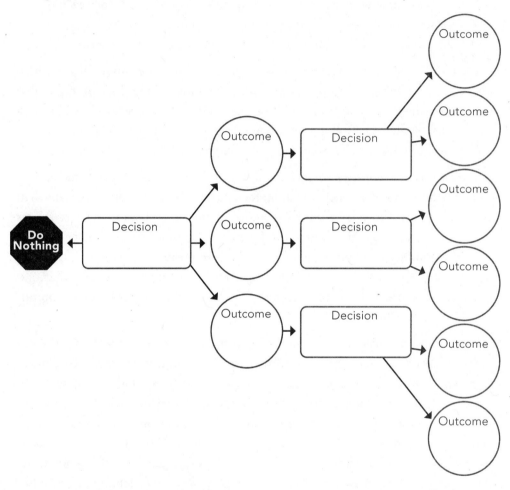

Figure 4.1: Decision tree template.

*Visit **go.SolutionTree.com/leadership** for a free reproducible version of this figure.*

Rachel, a former high school mathematics teacher and current education consultant, recalls a particular student who benefited from her having an open mind. Let's read about what she did and how it impacted the student's academic life.

> ### A Look at Leadership in a Classroom
>
> Rachel had a student, Eric, who constantly challenged her authority. Instead of asserting authority over him, she redirected when necessary and quietly observed his behavior. One day, as she was listening to a conversation between Eric and his buddy, she heard Eric talking about how he wanted to be in regular algebra 2 because he could be getting an A. Her class was the honors class, and he was getting a C. She finally had the answer to why he was acting so defiantly. Mathematics had naturally come easy to him his whole life. He was challenged by the material for the first time, and that made him uncomfortable. All of his acting out was to distract himself—and her—from the struggle he was experiencing with the content. She looked for ways to share power with Eric. As she did, his participation increased. One day, he engaged with the lecture by trying to contradict Rachel and prove that what she was saying was wrong. Rachel could have gotten angry, but instead she was excited for Eric. He was listening, and he was using his prior knowledge to make sense of a new concept. His argument wasn't correct, but he had deeper learning that day because he was free to question what she was saying. At the end of the semester, she wrote students personal notes of encouragement. Eric opened his right away. She told him that she appreciated that he doesn't accept everything he's told and that it's a strength to think independently and critically.

The key takeaway is that when you see a defiant behavior in students, it's tempting to interpret it as a negative because it's interrupting your plans, instruction, or expectations. But beneath that behavior could be a strength that would benefit these students and those with whom they interact in the future if you invite them to use that strength in your classes. By having an open mind, Rachel was able to recognize the positive in Eric's behavior and provide a safe space to learn and grow that strength.

Willingness to Adapt

The Center for Creative Leadership (2020) highlights the importance of flexibility and being adaptive, particularly throughout the COVID-19 pandemic and beyond: "Adaptability is about having ready access to a range of behaviors that enable leaders to shift and experiment as things change." Lacking that flexibility not only affects them, but those they lead. In fact, "inflexible leaders limit the adaptability of others. New initiatives may be halted or stifled" (Center for Creative Leadership, 2020). It's important for educational leaders to model being adaptive. Doing something just because *it's always been done that way* is the opposite of adaptive. Instead, how are you taking into account all the data to ensure the curriculum you are teaching is most beneficial to students? I don't just mean test scores—student interests and engagement should play significant roles in decision making as well. One strategy teachers can use to remain adaptive and flexible is through long-term planning. By planning entire units, you can begin with the end in mind. Educators and authors Grant Wiggins and Jay McTighe (2005) have written about backward planning in *Understanding by Design*, their seminal work about this subject. When teachers take the time to have that unit mapped out, they are able to adapt and adjust to student needs as they arise. That allows for some flexibility when the unexpected occurs. Successful instruction should be driven by student needs. The unit plan is merely that: a plan. Plans can be changed and modified as needed. You don't have to scrap the whole lesson, just make some adaptations to the unit plan, and keep moving.

Figure 4.2 shows how a third-grade teacher might plan out a unit about ecosystems while incorporating English language arts standards to learn about writing informative text.

Unit Plan for _____

Tentative dates _____

	Standard	Activity	Assessment
Week 1	Introduce a topic and group related information together; include illustrations when useful to aiding comprehension (W.3.2.A). Develop the topic with facts, definitions, and details (W.3.2.B).	The teacher will read aloud to students, introducing various ecosystems. The students will have time to explore various texts specific to ecosystems of their choice. The students will research their chosen ecosystem and take notes on a graphic organizer that the teacher has provided.	The students will write down their top three ecosystems that they want to learn more about. The students will complete at least half of their research by end of week.
Week 2	Develop the topic with facts, definitions, and details (W.3.2.B). Use linking words and phrases to connect ideas within categories of information (W3.2.C).	The students will continue researching and begin writing their informative text.	The students will complete their graphic organizers and begin their first drafts.

Week 3	Introduce a topic and group related information together; include illustrations when useful to aiding comprehension (W.3.2.A). Develop the topic with facts, definitions, and details (W.3.2.B). Use linking words and phrases to connect ideas within categories of information (W3.2.C). Provide a concluding statement or section (W3.2.D).	The students will complete their first draft and will begin publishing after a conference with the teacher.	The students will complete their first drafts and begin their final drafts.
Week 4	Introduce a topic and group related information together; include illustrations when useful to aiding comprehension (W.3.2.A). Develop the topic with facts, definitions, and details (W.3.2.B). Use linking words and phrases to connect ideas within categories of information (W3.2.C). Provide a concluding statement or section (W3.2.D).	The students will choose a method to demonstrate what they learned to their peers (such as a slide presentation, video, poster, or infographic).	The students will share their presentations with the class.

Source for standards: National Governors Association Center for Best Practices & Council of Chief State School Officers, 2010.

Figure 4.2: Unit plan template.

*Visit **go.SolutionTree.com/leadership** for a free reproducible version of this figure.*

Using the example in figure 4.2, the teacher could adapt in a number of ways depending on how the students are doing. He might shorten the unit to exclude the final project or by having the students write only one draft and using this as the evidence of learning. If students really get into the project, he might expand the unit by incorporating more drafts and widen the audience to include people outside of the classroom.

As both a teacher and a district administrator, I had plenty of practice at being flexible. Let's look at one instance during my years as an administrator.

> ### A Look at Leadership in a District
> In my early days as a curriculum director, I was charged with determining why our reading scores in grades K–4 were phenomenal, and then drastically fell at fifth grade and continued on a downward trend through graduation. I spent hours data mining, but I also talked with teachers and students. What I found to be the biggest factor was student choice, or rather, a lack thereof. Up until fifth grade, students were encouraged to read for pleasure, and at their level. Then, at fifth grade, the curriculum suddenly switched to a one-size-fits-all model. On top of that, I found that at the high school levels students had to get their pleasure reading materials approved by an English teacher. One student complained that he hated reading novels but loved reading his monthly subscription to *Field and Stream* magazine. The teacher, however, didn't deem it worthy. Something had to change. Adaptation was highly necessary. We began a communitywide reading initiative and school-based initiatives. We had to model and expect adaptive thinking in our principals, teachers, and parents. We didn't make huge curricular shifts right away but first sought to change the thinking around reading for enjoyment. We continued to adapt the curriculum over time, raising test scores and, more important, improving student engagement.

This story shows that flexibility doesn't mean making drastic changes overnight. Positive change is usually more sustainable when small steps are taken to set the plan in motion. Here, helping teachers have a more open mind toward pleasure reading had a ripple effect on the literacy of the entire district.

Failing Forward

Failing forward is a term coined by leadership guru John Maxwell (2000). It basically means you welcome mistakes, *adapt*, and learn from them. One might argue that this topic would better fit in chapter 6 on lifelong learners (page 69). But I'll counter that failing (and learning from it) first requires a good deal of flexibility. One must be open minded enough to embrace the flexibility necessary to benefit from failing. Bryan Goodwin, president and CEO of McREL International and author of *Balanced Leadership for Powerful Learning* (Goodwin & Cameron, 2015), wrote a 2017 article for *Educational Leadership* magazine called, "Personalization and Failing Forward." In it, he shares a story of his daughter taking on a personalized learning project. He speaks of the importance of embracing experimentation, reflection, and iteration (Goodwin, 2017). When leaders accept the necessity of being flexible to fail forward, they model that mentality to students. Students learn to practice that same mindset and become deeper critical thinkers because of it.

George, an elementary media specialist, remembers the moment in 2010 when the proverbial rug was pulled out from under him with a sudden position change. Let's look at how he used the worst moment in his professional life to fail forward, learning and growing in the process.

A Look at Leadership in a School

George was in his eighth year as an elementary media specialist and loved his job. He loved the school, the teachers, and most important, the students. On June 1, the last day the staff could be informed of position changes, the principal handed him an envelope with a letter welcoming him to the middle school. He was shocked and spent the summer feeling betrayed. He went as far as looking into jobs in other districts, but the pay cut that would have entailed left him feeling that he was stuck in his new position at the middle school.

In August, he realized that he was unprepared for his new job, as he'd used none of his time to gather information about the position, the school, and the available resources—a mistake that he knew would make him less effective—but he decided that he would make the best of the situation. He showed up to a new school where he knew no one and spoke honestly with the principal about his concerns. Fortunately, the principal was understanding and helped George ease into the new position.

At first, George was uncomfortable—he didn't have the same knowledge of the media for this age group, and it showed. He became discouraged but was determined to persevere. He started by reviewing the school's existing resources in a belated effort to build his knowledge. In doing so, George realized he had a unique opportunity to make some changes to a library that the staff had said was not being used. At his former school, the library had been central to building a love of reading in the students. Here, staff and students were not encouraged to use the resources as they were in the elementary school he'd worked at, and he decided that needed to change. George reached out to students and staff and made sure they knew they were welcome in the library. He got to know the students, talking sports with the reluctant readers and encouraging the strong readers to continue. It became cool to read in middle school. At the end of that year, the principal walked into George's office and asked him to close the door. He was there to thank him for making the library friendly again. He said that he was very happy with the changes George had made, and more important, he was glad the library was a happy, safe place again. George recognized that he'd made a mistake in failing to prepare for the new job, but he also knew that his effort to correct that mistake was what led to his insight about the library. He'd failed forward.

George could have decided to leave that district and find another elementary position, taking a pay cut so he could stay with what was comfortable and safe. Instead,
his persistent mindset and the caring leadership of his new principal allowed a poten-
tially horrible situation to turn into the best career move George says he's ever had.
He learned from his past experiences about how the library at the elementary school
had been used effectively and used this knowledge to make effective changes to benefit everyone at the middle school.

Table 4.1 shares ways leaders can demonstrate flexibility at the classroom, school,
and district levels.

Table 4.1: Leadership at a Glance—Strategies for Developing Flexibility

Focus Point	Leadership in a Classroom	Leadership in a School	Leadership in a District
An Open Mind	Many times, teachers don't get all of the background behind why decisions are made or new initiatives are adopted. It's important to keep an open mind that building and district leaders have the students' best interests in mind. When you assume good intentions, it's easier to be open minded, lending flexibility in moving forward.	Building leaders must be open minded to the ideas that come to them through parents, students, staff, and faculty. There are many stakeholders to hear from and opportunities to learn from them all. Listen to ideas and feedback and spend time reflecting before saying yes or no.	It's easy for district leaders to feel like they are carrying everything for the district. Teachers and building leaders, who are closer to the students, often have valuable insight that can help district administrators make more informed decisions. Having an open mind to their suggestions and garnering their input leads to a healthier organization as a whole.

Willingness to Adapt	Plan out units of study, rather than day-to-day lesson plans. Having a larger vision of where you want to go allows the time and space to be adaptive when students have ideas that might take you down a different path than that day's lesson plan. Some of the most authentic learning experiences happen organically in the classroom.	School delays, inclement weather, spur-of-the-moment school assemblies, and pandemics all cause a need for a building leader to demonstrate flexibility through adaptability. Having multiple plans of action in place allows leaders to adapt to the unknowns as they arise.	Not every initiative turns out the way it was planned. Sometimes, the best thing to do for a leader is to pivot. Being adaptive means knowing when to make changes, and even when to completely scrap a plan. That flexibility allows leaders to keep students and staff (not plans and initiatives) at the forefront of the work.
Failing Forward	Failing forward is all about keeping the growth mindset. When a lesson doesn't go according to plan, spend some time reflecting on why and make adjustments.	Just like having many stakeholders to hear from, building leaders have many stakeholders to learn from. Spending time reflecting on what has worked and hasn't worked (for both your school and others) allows building leaders to move forward into success.	Failing forward is a mindset that should be modeled by the district leaders. How can you practice reflective thinking in order to learn from what's happened? Reflection needs to be an intentional and regular practice for district leaders, so they can regularly learn and adjust.

Questions for Growth and Reflection

The following questions offer an opportunity to reflect on this chapter's content and think about what you might be able to work on.

1. When is a time that you had to change your mindset to be more open minded? How did it play out?
2. Where do you find it easiest to be adaptive? Where is the most challenging?
3. How can you model failing forward to those with whom you work?
4. What processes help you be more flexible?

CHAPTER 5

Leaders Have Integrity

I've had the privilege of working with many amazing educational leaders through-out my career. One stands out in my mind as a leader who always operated with clear integrity. Sandra Weaver, retired superintendent, took time to share a story with me about her experiences. Dr. Weaver is one of those highly respected educational leaders who recognizes how integrity in her personal life blends into her professional life. She generously shares a time of personal tragedy and how in the end, it bene-fited her students and staff:

> In November of 2011, my world imploded. After a week of intense headaches, my husband, Dave, was diagnosed with glioblastoma multiforme—Stage 4 brain cancer. He was referred to the Cleveland Clinic. After a day of appointments with oncologists and radiologists, we met with a neurosurgeon. She admitted him imme-diately and brain surgery was scheduled within two days. The night before the surgery, Dave told me he thought he was in the best place for a good outcome.
>
> The day of the surgery he and I and his two children accompanied him through a maze of corridors to the surgery prep area. The tech who pushed Dave's gurney told us we were in one of the most special hospitals in the world. He explained what to expect as we would wait during a 12-hour surgery. When we arrived in Dave's prep room we were met by the surgeon, the anesthesiologist, nurses, and a variety of surgical staff. In a choreographed routine, the surgeon directed each person to introduce themselves and state their role. She then introduced Dave and said his role was to relax as much as he could and be positive. She stated our roles were to be positive and to go the surgery waiting area. This was the start of an amazing journey led by the staff of the Cleveland Clinic.
>
> The surgical waiting area was enormous and had its own cafeteria. As I went to pay, the cashier asked what brought me there on this day. I broke into tears as I told him about Dave. He told me that the Cleveland Clinic was a world-renowned hospital. He went on to say that he had seen children after brain surgery, and

they were doing well. He said if surgeons here can do such delicate procedures on little ones, that surely my husband was in good hands.

Later during this long day, I wanted to walk off some anxiety and headed for a bookstore on the premises. I became disoriented and as I was looking for clues to its location, a gentleman asked if I needed directions. He gave them to me and then asked what brought me to the clinic. As I told him I began to sob. He gently moved me out of the traffic pattern of the corridor. He told me that the Cleveland Clinic was first internationally for heart surgery and third for brain surgery. As I calmed, he asked this question, "Are we being good to you here?" I said Dave and I and our family felt extremely comforted here and felt he was in the best place for this surgery.

In the day after Dave's surgery the nurses evaluated him and said it was time for the first test. They said I could help him stand up. Picture a small room with a man whose head is swathed in white bandages with a young woman mopping the floor on the other side of the room and two nurses watching. Dave was able to get up with my help and stand on his own. As he and I beamed at each other we heard clapping. The young woman mopping the floor had put her mop down and was gently applauding this momentous occasion. (S. Weaver, personal communication, October 1, 2020)

Sandra shared stories of service and care with Dave as he recuperated. Dave, an educator himself, pointed out that this experience was no accident; staff members must have received intensive training in customer service. They asked about it during a postoperative visit, and the neurosurgeon confirmed his assumption; she even said this commitment to customer service was so strong that the hospital's CEO told her that she would have to make time to attend the training or find another job.

Intrigued, Sandra called the Cleveland Clinic and asked for more information. She learned the hospital used a model known as Communicate With HEART, which is based on the assumption that all staff members, no matter their job title, are caregivers (Cleveland Clinic, n.d.). Although there was some pushback at first, people really bought into the idea that anyone could be a caregiver. Sandra quickly brought that training to her school district:

In a short time, our entire district staff was trained in the START with HEART model. Each school staff member is considered an educator. Consider the bus driver who instructs children on safety requirements, the cafeteria worker assisting children with manners and how to stand in line, the teacher who delivers curriculum, and the custodian who checks in with students about their homework. Every school staff member used the START communication style: **S**mile and greet warmly, **T**ell your name and role, **A**ctive listening, **R**apport and relationship building, and **T**hank the person. The HEART model is to **H**ear, **E**mpathize, **A**pologize, **R**espond, and **T**hank.

Dave lost his battle with cancer but was the impetus for a school district to change its communication style and lead with integrity in each and every conversation.

—Dedicated to Dr. David B. McGuire 5/30/47–3/7/13 (S. Weaver, personal communication, October 1, 2020)

Many education leaders, just like Sandra and Dave, find it difficult to separate the personal from the professional. When every single person they encountered at Cleveland Clinic modeled the same levels of care and integrity, they wanted to bring that to the students and staff members they served as educators. The hospital developed a program that models and teaches an attitude of caring and integrity for the entire organization. Hospital staff saw such benefit for the patients and families that they created a way to share this program with other organizations and in a way that can be customized regardless of industry. This saturation method of modeling carries consistency throughout the organization, providing clear communication and expectations. It pairs beautifully with schools and how educators at every level should interact with all stakeholders—with integrity as the guiding star. Part of the reason that Cleveland Clinic's model is so successful and translates so well to other organizations is that it charges every member of the organization to be a positive role model for others. We'll explore that idea in this chapter, along with the need to speak honestly and to deliver on promises with actions.

A Positive Role Model

Oxford Languages (n.d.) defines *integrity* as "the quality of being honest and having strong moral principles; moral uprightness." Educational leaders take integrity a step further by modeling those characteristics *with heart*, just as Sandra experienced throughout her husband's treatment. Leaders must act ethically even when it's not being observed, both acting with integrity and modeling it. Steven Mintz, expert on ethics, writes in a 2018 blog post, "Ethical leaders strive to honor and respect others in the organization and seek to empower others to achieve success by focusing on right action." This ties into the other leadership qualities we've discussed in earlier chapters. When leaders have integrity, it naturally builds a healthier culture, improving overall relationships in the organization. When the relationships are built, and the culture is positive, everyone can be more flexible and adapt to change more easily. Intuyu Consulting (2017) sums it up quite nicely: "Simply put, lack of integrity makes causing change (or even transformation) that much harder."

In an *Edutopia* article, "Creating a Culture of Integrity in the Classroom," developmental psychologist and researcher Marilyn Price-Mitchell (2015) writes about the importance of modeling integrity at all levels. She points out that children aren't born with ethical qualities. She writes:

> In their school environments, students acquire these values and behaviors from adult role models and peers, and in particular, through an understanding of the principles of academic integrity. When students learn integrity in classroom settings, it helps them apply similar principles to other aspects of their lives. (Price-Mitchell, 2015)

Educators can model integrity in these key ways.

- **Make integrity a classroom norm:** Many teachers spend countless hours at the beginning of each school year establishing norms and expectations. By using language about ethics and integrity, teachers can show the students that they value those characteristics in that classroom. A statement such as, "Be honest with yourself and others" shows students that honesty is important in the classroom. This also underpins anti-cheating measures while keeping a positive focus on acting with integrity.

- **Establish consistent consequences for student behavior:** Teacher and building leaders both need to be consistent regarding the consequences students receive for unethical behavior. Through this consistency, the students will feel safer and more understanding of what is expected, which continues to support the positive school culture.

- **Help students believe in themselves:** Price-Mitchell (2015) notes, "When young people learn to believe in themselves, dishonesty and disrespect no longer make much sense. Living with integrity becomes a way of life." When teachers have formed authentic relationships with students, they are able to draw on student interests, passions, and strengths to help them find success. When teachers demonstrate a level of knowledge about students, they can help students flourish. Showing they believe in the students helps the students believe in themselves each time they experience small wins in the classroom.

Figure 5.1 guides you through a series of reflective questions for an integrity self-needs assessment.

John Robinson (2013), school administrator, writes, "By our demonstrations of integrity, we communicate to those who follow us that integrity is important." Modeling the desired behavior, mindset, and practices is one of the best things a leader can do. This goes beyond moral behavior. The actions of leaders are not only linked to the leaders' integrity but the integrity of the organization they represent. For example, if teachers are supposed to be using engaging technology tools in their classrooms, then the principal should be learning about new resources and strategies and employing them during staff meetings. If a superintendent wants the principals to be present

Describe your thoughts on each reflective question as it relates to you as a leader.	
When you are honest or show integrity, how do you feel?	
What does it feel like when people treat you with integrity?	
Are there times when it is difficult for you to show integrity? Give an example.	
Who do you think is responsible for you being honest and showing integrity? Why?	
Do you think controlling what you do and say is a way to show integrity? How?	
Is there a common theme that rises from your answers?	
Is there an integrity-based goal that would help you grow as a leader?	

Figure 5.1: Integrity self-needs assessment.

*Visit **go.SolutionTree.com/leadership** for a free reproducible version of this figure.*

during extracurricular activities, then the district administrators need to attend these events periodically as well. When a "do as I do" mentality expands throughout the school system, it translates into a positive mindset in the staff, from the district offices to the classrooms.

Elementary school teacher Courtney Curtis (2019) writes, "Teaching students how to treat others and how to react in situations and conflict is something I try and do each and every day." This mindset represents how a leader with integrity operates. When the focus is doing whatever you're supposed to do to the best of your ability, you'll be modeling that practice for every stakeholder.

Mark is a seasoned educational leader who has seen an evolution in leadership style since he entered the workforce in the early 1980s. The changes have mostly been for the better as leaders have become more positive role models. He recounts one of the more traditional leaders he had early on.

> **A Look at Leadership in a District**
>
> Mark's first superintendent always wore a suit, commanded respect, and demanded loyalty. He very much wanted to be the "smartest person in the room." This mindset led to a disjointed team that he ran through fear rather than a collaborative spirit. High turnover in that administrative team came as no surprise to Mark as he watched leader after leader leave due to the superintendent's command-and-control nature. After Mark left that district, he found himself on a district leadership team where his new superintendent modeled a humble, team-oriented outlook. From the way the superintendent spoke to his team to the way he conducted himself in the community, he demonstrated what it is to have integrity. As a result, the team was cohesive and eager to work together for the good of the organization.

The key takeaway in this story comes back to the leadership style modeled by both superintendents. One was not a positive role model and was in turn ineffective, while the other bore the hallmark of a healthy culture because of the integrity modeled by the top leader in the district.

Honesty

A large part of integrity is being honest, which begins with being honest with yourself and recognizing your weaknesses. Sinek (2012) asserts, "Knowing how to talk about our weaknesses, it turns out, can be one of our greatest strengths." Being honest with yourself must come before you can operate honestly in your position. Leaders need to know when to ask for help. In the classroom, this could look like asking a student to help you learn a new digital resource. At the building and district levels, maybe you create a team of thought partners that brings people with different skills to the table, especially honesty. You want to foster a culture where stakeholders feel comfortable being honest with you, otherwise the help you receive will be disingenuous.

Another way to nurture honesty in the organization is take responsibility for mistakes that you make. Showing how you reflect on and learn from mistakes demonstrates that you are being honest with yourself and those you serve. That transparency is identified as vital by K–12 leadership experts Jill Berkowicz and Ann Myers (2017) in their article, "Trust in Our Schools Requires Honesty and Good Communication." They write:

> If we are to gain momentum and gather a community of support, trust is the essential element. Trust building depends upon things like keeping your word, taking time when making decisions, valuing others, honesty, being authentic, doing what is right and a most important attribute to develop in concert with these others is to be good communicators. (Berkowicz & Myers, 2017)

We need trust and honesty to build relationships. We need relationships to sustain change. And all of that is built on the backbone of leader integrity.

I had the privilege of working with a very talented high school teacher in Texas. Joe teaches computer technology, computer maintenance, and futures in science, technology, engineering, and mathematics (STEM). Let's see how being honest with students and creating a culture of risk-taking leads to more engaged learning.

A Look at Leadership in a Classroom

One semester, Joe decided to implement a Genius Hour time for his students. It was a huge success. He had many students asking when the next project could begin, with several planning on furthering the work they started earlier. He was reflecting on how great it would be if every day could be Genius Hour. He realized by giving his students honest support and feedback throughout the project as well as freedom to try new things and take new risks, that they were more highly engaged than ever before. He still held students accountable for their learning, and he could still ensure that they were learning the state standards and curriculum. The difference was that the students were using critical and creative thinking skills like never before. They were working on real-world applications to the knowledge, skills, and concepts they acquired during their study time. Plus, it made him available to teach personalized minilessons in the moment.

Joe's students could see that taking risks was not only accepted but encouraged as a way to learn and grow, and they welcomed his honest approach to feedback. They knew feedback from him would be authentic and helpful in furthering their thinking. That freedom for experimentation led the students to take ownership over their own learning, and they also responded positively to the fact that he delivered on his promise to let them have more freedom, which is another important part of leadership integrity.

Promises to Actions

Educational leaders make a multitude of decisions daily, but some are not always clear cut. John Robinson (2013), writer and school administrator, addresses the importance of educational leaders having integrity in his blog post for *The 21st Century Principal*. He writes, "Personal agendas become the drivers of decisions made, often at the expense of 'rightness,' and standing up for what is right is not the most advantageous, politically correct thing to do" (Robinson, 2013).

Leaders must be careful that their actions reflect doing what is best for the students first. These choices may not always be the most politically sound, but acting with integrity means putting personal agendas aside. For example, creating a no-homework policy may not be popular with teachers, but doing so could be what is best for students; there is a growing body of research that indicates homework doesn't help students learn and may just create stress (Walker, 2019). Brené Brown (2018), speaker and author, writes, "Integrity is choosing courage over comfort; it's choosing what's right over what's fun, fast or easy; and it's practicing your values, not just professing them" (p. 227). This is where the actions of leaders must match the values they profess.

Christine, a former high school principal, had to find ways to maintain her own integrity even when faced with a boss whose values and actions didn't match hers. She was able to support her students and staff through her own actions despite the adversity.

A Look at Leadership in a School

For a short period of time, Christine worked in a small school district with a history of local control that resulted in the school progressing in some areas while falling behind in others. She and the superintendent agreed on several future outcomes, but during her first year she quickly learned that their individual approaches to actualize those outcomes were drastically different. With trends indicating a dwindling student population for at least the next four years, they needed a plan that helped both strengthen their instructional program and preclude overstaffing.

Christine brought the dilemma to the leadership team and asked for team members to work together to come up with their most creative ideas. They explored everything from master schedule adjustments, to curriculum redesign, to the launch and promotion of innovative programs that would bring more families into their community. The superintendent, however, took a more drastic and shocking approach: without first discussing it with the schools' principals, he announced the reduction in force of sixteen staff members during a public budget meeting. This was difficult for Christine, as a principal, to recover from because she recognized the pride the community took in the school and the prominent role it played as an employment agency in a struggling community—plus she had trusted that the staff would find and implement a solution. The staff members no longer trusted the superintendent to look after their learners because he didn't include them in seeking alternatives.

It took significant self-restraint for Christine not to stand in front of the community that night and pronounce the superintendent unstable and self-serving. She realized that would have only created deeper divisions, and they already had a lot of healing to do. Instead, they rallied together as a team and continued to drive forward with their mission to serve the students of the community. This focus helped them adjust to the outcome they might not have believed was the best solution.

Maybe we haven't all been faced with the same situation Christine was with her superintendent, but we can all learn from her story by realizing that we can only control our own actions and should control them even if they don't match those in other leadership positions.

Table 5.1 shares ways leaders can demonstrate being positive role models, speak honestly, and deliver on their promises with appropriate action.

Table 5.1: Leadership at a Glance—Strategies for Developing Integrity

Focus Point	Leadership in a Classroom	Leadership in a School	Leadership in a District
A Positive Role Model	Include the students in setting the norms and expectations for the room and then follow them and follow through.	Model the expectations you have for the teachers. If you want them increasing the use of technology with their students, then find ways to increase the use of technology during staff meetings and communications.	Being visible and showing teachers and building leaders that you are invested in the students is the best way to be a positive role model in the district. Read to kindergartners, attend band concerts, guest teach in middle school classes, and so on.
Honesty	Be honest with students, who are the best lie detectors, and don't be afraid of admitting when you don't know something.	Speak with truth, and stay consistent. This goes a long way in the relational trust that principals need to build with both students and staff.	Be true to your word, and stay consistent in the messaging provided to parents, students, staff, and board members.
Promises to Actions	Help students discover and discuss their own values. This will help you hold yourself accountable for your actions as well as guide their choices.	Make sure your actions match your words. This is true for what you say to students and staff and how you follow through.	Ensure that the district has clearly defined core values and then never ask anyone to act in violation to the district's vision and values.

Questions for Growth and Reflection

The following questions offer an opportunity to reflect on this chapter's content and think about what you might be able to work on.

1. How do you define integrity?

2. What are the vision and values of your school or district? How do they align with your belief system?

3. When is a time that you had to be honest with yourself or others about a mistake you'd made?

4. What is one action you want to take to better practice integrity in leadership?

CHAPTER 6

Leaders Are Lifelong Learners

Are you a lifelong learner? It's a term educators often use and a quality we hope to instill in our learners, but are we, as leaders, modeling this value? All good teachers and leaders see the importance of continual growth. Danielle Gagnon (2019) of Southern New Hampshire University interviewed university education faculty and students and asked them what traits effective teachers had in common. Of her findings, she writes, "Whether you're learning more about your subject area, learning new methods of communication or even exploring how to bring more technology into your classroom, continuing to expand your own knowledge is key to expanding that of your students" (Gagnon, 2019).

Leaders must make time to feed their own learning to stay relevant and effective. Leaders must be the models of what they expect to see in their teammates. We are never done learning. Noa Daniel, teacher, consultant at Building Outside the Blocks, and co-founder of The Mentoree, agrees whole-heartedly with this sentiment. She has seen the impact of continuous learning in her own practice as an educator and in her growth as a leader:

> A decade ago, after fourteen years of teaching at the same school, I was excited to have been offered a job at an independent school that was part of the International Baccalaureate. While I wasn't totally sure what that meant when I accepted, it felt like a new path and a way to intensify my learning and teaching practice. The IB uses inquiry-based learning and is about depth over breadth. It's grounded in the notion that we can all have different ideas while being simultaneously right. It was a challenge to learn how to shift my practice, but it was an even greater challenge to navigate these new waters.

> When I first started there, I noticed that the other new teachers were given time with our curriculum coach, so I asked to be slotted in. My head of school said that I was too seasoned a practitioner, and that I didn't need her. He told me that I was hired to be a leader in the school and that leaders like me did not need the

support of a coach. I respectfully disagreed with him, arguing that the new context and the shift to IB would necessitate some level of mentorship/coaching, and time with this individual could only positively support my work at the school. While I believe that new teachers require the most support when they begin their careers, at no point in a career or life, especially not in a teaching career, does learning end. If we are always learning, then wouldn't any person at any stage of their career really need the support of a mentor/coach? While I didn't argue this particular point, my head of school did acquiesce based on my other points, and I started meeting Ricki every week for a half hour for the next 3 years.

Ricki extended my thinking. In our sessions, we would discuss the TED talks she encouraged me to watch, articles on education she had shared, and how I approached some of my unit planning. Her many questions, in turn, got me asking a lot of questions about my work. Before I had watched or read about Simon Sinek [2009], she got me asking about my golden circle. I asked why, how, and what as well as so what and now what about my professional learning and practice. Her questions helped me discover that I had unknowingly developed an entire teaching approach that positively impacted my students and was totally unique on the education landscape.

Ricki coached and mentored me through some of the challenges I was facing at this new school and to becoming a better educator. As Dr. James Comer [1995] said, "No significant learning can occur without a significant relationship." Mentorship is also about relationships, and my relationship with Ricki and the subsequent mentors, both formal and informal, that I would learn to seek have been transformational. Leaders are lifelong learners, so they need to know how they learn best in order to ensure that.

I learned many things about myself through my mentorship experience with Ricki, but one of the enduring lessons was that I learned better when I had the support of a mentor. It helps me in my professional learning, sense of well-being about my work, and my efficacy toward my work. Mentorship is a powerful tool for learning and leadership. It is a gift I hope to repay and pay forward through my work in mentorship for educators at any and every stage of their career. (N. Daniel, personal communication, October 7, 2020)

Like Noa's boss, one of the biggest mistakes leaders make is not attending to their own growth. Leaders often see the need for continuous learning but spend available time and money on their employees and not on their own growth. Or they might attend a conference that is specific to their market but not necessarily to their growth as a leader. The best professional learning experiences are personalized for the learner and not a one-size-fits-all approach. This chapter will look at how leaders can drive personal growth by goal setting and self-reflection.

Personal Growth

I have heard numerous educators complain about professional development over the years. The school principal will pick a book for a schoolwide book study. A superintendent will invite a keynote speaker to address the entire district. Faculty meetings are used for housekeeping items that could have been in an email. Teachers attend a conference and choose to sit in sessions that they don't find relevant to their own needs. Most of the time, these opportunities are born of good intent. But just like in the classroom, there is no one-size-fits-all approach when it comes to learning.

Many people use these experiences as a reason to complain and justify their lack of learning or growth. As adults who have a calling to serve the students in our classrooms, schools, and districts, this excuse isn't valid. We are responsible for driving our own growth.

Joseph Lathan (n.d.), program director at the University of San Diego, identifies his top leadership qualities in his article, "10 Traits of Successful School Leaders." He agrees that being a lifelong learner is one of those ten traits. He writes, "Perhaps the most important of all qualities that a school leader can possess is the unquenchable thirst for knowledge" (Lathan, n.d.). That thirst will look different for most people, just as learning can look different for every person. The key is to seek out learning for which you have a personal passion.

Leaders who are lifelong learners find ways to learn something new, a way to challenge thinking, people who push them further, and books that add value for them personally and professionally. I most frequently learn through reading (articles, books, tweets, and blog posts), but I am most energized by learning from peers in person. I have colleagues who prefer learning via podcasts or webinars. There is no *right* way. Find what works best with your lifestyle and what you enjoy most.

Driving your own growth begins with a self-needs assessment. This can be something formal that you work through, or it can be a time spent reflecting through writing or conversing with a trusted peer. Start by identifying areas of strength. These can be work related, but you should also look at personality traits as well. Remembering names well, being able to quickly build rapport, having a quick wit, enjoying a good book—these can all translate into professional strengths. Then, identify areas of need. Be real and be deep in this assessment. Sometimes the needs you identify will correspond with school or district initiatives. From that assessment, identify one need that you want to focus on first and start creating a growth plan that will challenge you, but also be enjoyable along the way, identifying the people and resources that can help support that growth.

Figure 6.1 borrows the well-known ideas of what you must know, understand, and be able to do (Tomlinson, 2017) and goals that are strategic and specific, measurable, attainable, results oriented, and time bound (SMART; Conzemius & O'Neill, 2014). It provides a goal-setting, implementation, and reflection template to guide your pursuit of professional growth. You can establish whatever time line works best for your learning.

A Guide for Goal Setting, Action, and Reflection	
Reflective Planning	
What are my current school or district goals?	
What are the areas I get most excited about or interested in (professionally or personally)?	
What do I most want to know, understand, and be able to do in order to be a better leader?	
SMART Goal *Strategic and specific, measurable, attainable, results oriented, and time bound*	
Sample format: In order to _____, I will _____. I will monitor my progress toward this goal by_____.	
What resources will I need to help me achieve my goal? (Record people, tools, media, and so on)	
What experiences might I need to develop new understanding or skills?	

Action Plan

What is one step I can take immediately to initiate action to make progress toward my goal? What other next steps can occur independently in addition to this?

Date	Item to Accomplish

Reflective Cycle

Set aside time weekly to reflect on your progress. This can be done independently, with a coach, or with a trusted colleague. After reflecting, add next steps to your action plan.

Date:	Reflections:
Date:	Reflections:
Date:	Reflections:

Figure 6.1: Goals and implementation framework.

*Visit **go.SolutionTree.com/leadership** for a free reproducible version of this figure.*

Dawn, a curriculum director, shares how one of her favorite resources for professional growth is Twitter and the bonds she has formed through it.

A Look at Leadership in a District

Dawn is one of those educators who truly loves to learn. Twitter has become her go-to learning platform. Her favorite part about it is that she can jump on for a few minutes and instantly find great blog posts, resource ideas, or encouraging words from other educational leaders and professionals. It is the easiest way for her to get her learning fix. The wonderful side benefit is the personal learning network (PLN) she has established through social media. The best part is that social media allows her to enlarge her PLN beyond school walls and city limits. She has found that learning with and from her PLN is one of the easiest ways to grow. After engaging in a conversation via Twitter, Dawn feels energized, excited, and typically eager to take another step in her own growth.

As leaders, we can gather from Dawn's story that growth can, and should, take on more forms than just learning in the traditional sense. Learning should be fun and beneficial. Will it always be beneficial? Yes. We either learned something from the experience or learned that we won't have that kind of experience again. All learning should produce some type of change. It could be major or minor, but some thoughts and actions should be challenged, affirmed, or stretched based on every learning experience. And we know that generally change is hard to prepare for. The most we can do to prepare is to be open minded, attentive, and in a constant state of learning and growth.

Goal Setting

I was a classroom teacher for fourteen years. I enjoyed the work and genuinely cared about my students. What I didn't realize was that around the thirteen-year mark, I was slowly approaching the burn-out phase. It wasn't until I became the district's curriculum director that my passion for education was reignited, alerting me to the fact that the fire for teaching had dimmed over the most recent few years of my time in the classroom. Through job-embedded coaching, I've had the opportunity to help multiple principals establish goals for themselves and their schools. Let's look at three of those principals and how setting goals impacted them, their teachers, and their students.

A Look at Leadership in a School

Ben invested two years in building capacity in his school for transforming instruction to be more student-driven. His teachers showed tremendous buy-in, and, therefore, the growth was enormous. His goal became to take this a step further to work toward personalized learning. His first step centered around project-based learning. He wanted his students to be able to construct their own questions, conduct their own research, and own their own learning. He saw how blended learning experiences and project-based learning enhanced their understanding of their own growth and learning progress.

His colleague, Colby, wanted to enable his students to be responsible digital citizens. He recognized the importance of intentional teaching to ensure his students knew how to conduct valid searches, find reliable resources, establish a positive digital legacy, and maintain safety in the digital environment.

Camille, an elementary principal, saw the value of increasing communication and collaboration skills among her students. She planned to work with her teacher leadership team to model strategies and tools that they can take back to their teams to use in the classroom.

All leaders have a different goal, a different vision for their staff and students. The commonality among each of them, however, is their passion for what they do. They value every stakeholder in their buildings and remain dedicated to the work that educators do. They are each continual learners, which is what makes the cultures in their buildings so strong. The common mindset of setting goals is what drives the progress in each of their schools.

Many schools and districts require their educators to write goals. Unfortunately, many goals are vague, and little follow-up occurs after the initial goal setting. Josh Bowen (2018), founder of 3×5 Leadership, writes, "Goal-setting can be an effective tool for leaders to provide challenge, focus, and motivation to their people. Unfortunately, this tool is often underutilized or poorly implemented." Goals should be clear and shared with someone.

There are five basic keys to driving personal growth through goals.

1. **Write a SMART goal:** The first known use of the SMART acronym occurs in an article by George T. Doran in the November 1981 issue of *Management Review* (Doran, 1981). Anne E. Conzemius and Jan O'Neill (2014) contribute important thinking about the use of SMART goals in education settings. The most important part of the goal for growth is the *measurable* part. It makes the goal more focused and less likely to be something vague. I once had a teacher write, "To measure my progress, I will

watch my students grow in their problem-solving skills." How do you do that? I can't focus on growth efforts or reflect on progress when I don't know what I'm measuring. A way to improve that goal would be, "To measure progress, I will pose inquiry-based questions to increase my students' critical-thinking skills once per week, using a rubric to measure their growth. One hundred percent of my students will respond on Webb's (2002) Depth of Knowledge at a level three or four at least once per month."

2. **Write two to three immediate action steps with dates as deadlines:** These action steps are just as important to learning and growth as the actual goal. As soon as the goal is written (and often, revised), write two or three things that you will do that will immediately aid in working toward that goal—and then put deadlines beside them. It is far too easy to write a goal and then get slammed with everything else so that you become too busy to actually start working on that goal. The action steps are what will initially drive the growth. This is the first step to creating an action plan and the first step to new learning.

3. **Share them with someone, ideally a coach:** Accountability partners work for a reason. Every educator, at every level, can benefit from working with a coach. If you are fortunate enough to have a coach to work with, then share your goal document with them. If not, find a trusted colleague to be your person. They can be as involved or not as you want. The purpose is having that goal out there in the world so that you hold yourself more accountable. This person should be invested enough to ask you about your goal and/or action steps on a regular basis.

4. **Schedule times for intentional reflection:** Reflection is *the most important* aspect of driving personal growth. I have found that for me, if it's not written on the calendar, it just doesn't happen at the level deep enough to cause change and growth. This is a time to be deeply real with yourself. Ideally, this happens with that coach or trusted colleague. The coach or colleague does not even have to drive the conversation, just be a place for you to talk, think, and process what's happening. What successes have you experienced? What challenges are still there? What can you change, learn, try to keep moving forward?

5. **Set more action steps:** That reflection time is what helps you form the next set of action steps. Growth can only occur if you continue reflecting, learning, and moving forward. These action steps are the propellant.

These five steps help drive personal growth, but the desire must first be there. None of us should ever feel like we have learned all we need to learn. The desire to continue learning and growing is what keeps the excitement fresh and the passion alive.

Self-Reflection

When I was a classroom teacher, I tended to reflect on the fly. I'd take a quick assessment and make adjustments on teaching materials, strategies, and temperature of the class. I'd either reteach or make notes for changes for the following year. When I attended professional learning opportunities, I'd often reflect through the conversations I had with colleagues at the event or after I returned to school. I rarely spent a lengthy amount of time during the reflection process.

When I moved into the role of curriculum director, I recognized a need to make this process more intentional. The role was brand new, and I was forging it as I went. I decided that the easiest way for me to make intentional time for reflection would be to schedule it every Monday and to reflect through writing. This worked for me since it only involved me, and I wasn't dependent on another person having the same time free to talk. In those early days, my reflection often centered around new knowledge or practices I was learning to be better in my new role. Later, it morphed into including reflecting on the programs I was developing, initiatives I was implementing, or strategies I was introducing to the teachers and administrators in my district.

I firmly believe that everyone benefits from intentional reflection. As leaders, we want students to reflect on their learning, so we need to do the same.

Janet, a retired kindergarten teacher, reflects on a particular time in her career where her learning and reflection on programming positively impacted her students.

A Look at Leadership in a Classroom

During Janet's thirty-five years of teaching kindergarten, there were constant changes that affected her classroom strategies as well as the students' learning experiences. When she began teaching kindergarten in 1979, her school did not provide any materials or curriculum guides. The following year, she used The Letter People (inflatable characters to represent each letter of the alphabet) for daily lessons and activities to help students with letter recognition as well as language skills. Even though she enjoyed teaching with The Letter People, after attending a professional development workshop and reflecting on what she learned there, she soon realized that The Letter People did not allow her students to reach the potential that other techniques provided. It was during that intentional reflection that she realized The Letter People used the entire year to focus on letters but did not guide the students to actual reading.

Janet implemented a new program that focused on the students' names. This provided a more personalized approach for each student. As students observed their name or the names of fellow classmates, they learned to recognize the letters

continued ▶

in the whole name, letter shapes, tall letters, short letters, and how letters worked together to form words and then to build sentences. This approach led to a whole reading experience. Soon students could read or recognize the names of their classmates as well as their own. When she asked them the question, "What do you notice about this name?" all students could be successful with their observations. They could count how many letters it took to make a certain name, note similarities and differences in names, cheer for individual names, and put names of classmates in alphabetical order. Using this approach, students quickly began reading and building sentences.

With this beginning, students could progress more readily and not spend an entire year basically learning to name and recognize letters. Janet experienced a new learning technique, and she was able to observe more methods for success. In Janet's classroom, it changed her teaching, and, more importantly, it changed the learning of her kindergartners.

There are three main takeaways from Janet's experience that we can use to drive our own reflection and personal growth, as well.

1. **Mindset matters:** We want our students to have a growth mindset, but how often do we experience it with our teachers? Janet did just that. She spent hours developing lessons around one program, then spent hours in a professional development workshop learning about a new approach. She spent time reflecting on her current work and how it was impacting her students. She may have been frustrated and overwhelmed, but she kept working and learning because of the mindset she had to provide the best experiences possible for her students.

2. **Learning can be both challenging and fun:** Janet was definitely challenged throughout her career. She made it a point, however, to find fun ways to learn and to teach her students in a way that was best for them.

3. **Limitation is a state of mind:** Janet didn't complain about a lack of curriculum or resources. She just sat down and got to work learning how to make the most out of what she did have to best benefit the students that walked through her doors each day. She didn't see limitations; she saw opportunities for learning.

How often do you allow your students to fail and see it as a good thing? How often do you let yourself have that same freedom? It is through failed ideas, trials, and projects that we all become stronger learners. Your ideas are clarified. Your trials move to the next phase. Your projects are improved. So why does the term *failure* contain such a negative connotation? Ed Catmull (2014), cofounder of Pixar, writes in his book *Creativity, Inc.: Overcoming the Unseen Forces That Stand in the Way of True Inspiration*, "Failure *is* a manifestation of learning and exploration" (p. 109). How can you promote and embrace a growth mindset to see that truth? By setting aside time for intentional reflection both for yourself and for students, you can explore and learn through setbacks and failures. You can learn how to pivot and ideate to find solutions that are better than what you might have come to otherwise.

Be the driver of your own growth. Realize that, at times, you will be expected to attend a training the school or district requires. Go with a good attitude. It will be more enjoyable and beneficial for all involved. Be the learner you want your students to be. To build a positive culture that results in a strong organization, leaders need to take time to build relationships, plan strategically, incorporate reflective practice, and maintain an attitude of continuous learning.

Table 6.1 shares ways leaders can model being lifelong learners by driving their own growth, setting goals, and scheduling time for intentional reflection.

Table 6.1: Leadership at a Glance—Strategies for Lifelong Learning

Focus Point	Leadership in a Classroom	Leadership in a School	Leadership in a District
Personal Growth	Consider modeling your needs assessment in front of your students. This will show them how to take charge of their own learning journey.	Consider modeling your needs assessment in front of your teachers. This will show them that you are a lifelong learner and demonstrate your willingness to be vulnerable with your staff, which promotes a healthier culture.	Consider modeling your needs assessment in front of your district team. This will help you maintain a line of sight on the district's vision and mission and demonstrate your willingness to be vulnerable with your colleagues, which promotes a healthier culture.
Goal Setting	Use the SMART goal format to determine a specific and clarified goal that will enable you to set detailed action steps toward success. Find one colleague to share your goal with.	Use the SMART goal format to determine a specific and clarified goal that will enable you to set detailed action steps toward success. Find one colleague to share your goal with.	Use the SMART goal format to determine a specific and clarified goal that will enable you to set detailed action steps toward success. Find one colleague to share your goal with.

continued ▶

Focus Point	Leadership in a Classroom	Leadership in a School	Leadership in a District
Self-Reflection	Schedule time for self-reflection, which can be anywhere from five minutes to thirty minutes depending on where your thoughts go. Schedule during a time that you can keep separate and not be rushed.	Model self-reflection time for staff during, for example, a faculty meeting. This demonstrates the importance of the process, while ensuring you have set apart time to do it. Make sure you finish the reflection by writing concrete next steps into your action plan.	Schedule self-reflection time with an accountability partner. If this is difficult to schedule on a regular basis at the same time with your accountability partner, write out your reflections at the same time each week, and share those thoughts with your partner. This ensures that you stay true to the intentionality of your reflection and allows your accountability partner time to respond in between.

Questions for Growth and Reflection

The following questions offer an opportunity to reflect on this chapter's content and think about what you might be able to work on.

1. With whom will you share your goals?

2. What day or time each week will you carve out for intentional reflection?

3. What feelings do you experience when a trusted colleague challenges you on your growth?

4. What resources will help you most in accomplishing your goals?

5. How will your goals benefit the students or teachers in your care?

Conclusion

L eadership is not just a position in the central office or a title you have. Hopefully, after reading this book, you feel empowered as an educational leader in whatever your current role may be. Often, teachers feel like administrators are disconnected from the classroom, and administrators feel like teachers don't understand their responsibilities each day. This book was designed to give educators at every level insight into leadership in the classroom, the schools, and the entire district. Knowing how to support one another also helps you grow in your own leadership journey.

This book is all about strengthening those five main qualities of effective leadership. Leaders in any capacity have the responsibility to continue to learn and grow. Without that continuous pursuit for improvement, leaders can become stagnant and less effective. There are different actions you can all take along your path of leadership development. Here are ten quick takeaways to add to the learning you already did through the previous chapters.

1. **Drive your own growth:** Leaders can't afford to wait around for the organization to provide their professional learning opportunities. Everyone is responsible for their own personal growth plan. So, first, determine areas of opportunity for growth. What do you want to learn? How do you want to grow? This is designed and owned by you.

2. **Get connected:** With so many social media sites, it's easy to find other educators and leaders. It's not enough to just connect, however. Leaders should foster those relationships through authentic interactions and conversations. So, take time to interact with posts as well as initiate and respond to direct messages. Those conversations will definitely add to your growth, and you never know what opportunities may arise because of them.

3. **Set goals:** Not only do leaders need to set realistic and personal goals but they need to write them down, keep them visible, and share them

with someone to hold them accountable. Goals should be attainable but still stretch you. The beauty of designing and owning your own growth plan is that goals can be flexible. Feel free to tweak those as needs or opportunities change.

4. **Learn:** How are you feeding your growth? Continuous learning has never been easier. Find the right people to learn with and from and then also tap into all the resources at your fingertips: podcasts, blog posts, books, articles, webinars, videos—the list is endless. The important part is that you are finding the ways and places to learn and grow toward accomplishing your goals.

5. **Reflect:** Setting goals and creating a learning pathway are vital to leadership development, but without intentional reflection leaders can lose much of their growth potential. Set aside time weekly to reflect. If it's not on the schedule, it likely won't happen. I actually put reflection time on my calendar each week. It doesn't matter if you do this individually, or if you find someone to reflect with. The point is to do it. Reflect on the learning and reflect on your growth toward your goal.

6. **Create an action plan:** Writing a goal is necessary, but after that is established, you still have to create an action plan. Writing down specific steps with due dates helps craft the plan that will help you accomplish your goals. Revisit the action plan each week during your reflection time. Did you accomplish each step? What next steps do you need to take? The action plan is dynamic and continuously growing until the goal is accomplished.

7. **Find a coach:** Who helps you through your journey of leadership development? It doesn't matter if you've been in the field for twenty years or one year. A coach is vital to your growth and success. Coaching can happen 100 percent virtually, so there is nothing stopping you from finding that person to support, encourage, and challenge you along the way. If you are fortunate enough to have a coach in your building or district, volunteer to work with this coach. If you don't, you can ask a trusted colleague (in person or virtually), to serve as a coach. Lastly, there are professional coaches who work with educational leaders every day who could support your growth.

8. **Invite feedback:** To grow, leaders must be open to other peoples' perspectives. You must invite feedback and then be open to how you might apply that feedback along your pathway for growth. If you don't have a growth mindset, you won't grow. It's that simple. Invite people in to watch a lesson, proofread districtwide correspondence, read through your mission statement, and anything else you can think of. Good feedback allows you to stretch and grow.

9. **Take care of yourself:** How do you take care of yourself? There are things that I make sure I do daily, weekly, and monthly to refill my bucket. For me, I have to find time each day for physical activity and connecting with my kids. I try to eat healthy throughout the day and disconnect from work in the evenings. I don't check work emails on the weekend if I can help it. It doesn't matter what it looks like, just make sure you are taking care of yourself. That's the only way to be the best leader you can be.

10. **Repeat the cycle for continuous growth:** Once you have accomplished one goal, it's time to write a new one and craft a new action plan. Learning and growth should never stop.

The best part about leadership is that everyone can strengthen their own leadership capacity. Learning never stops, and growth can be continual. Great leaders have many common qualities. They are relational, innovative, flexible, have integrity, and are lifelong learners in thinking and leading. To be successful, leaders need to be an equal and empower the staff that works for them. Leaders can't lead by themselves. Share the vision, and help others get on board by modeling the importance of continued growth and mutual respect.

References and Resources

Baker, E. L., Dunne-Moses, A., Calarco, A. J., & Gilkey, R. (2019). Listening to understand: A core leadership skill. *Journal of Public Health Management and Practice, 25*(5), 508–510. Accessed at https://journals.lww.com/jphmp/Fulltext/2019/09000/Listening_to_Understand__A_Core _Leadership_Skill.13.aspx,%2010.1097/phh.0000000000001051 on October 14, 2019.

Becker, B. (2021, May 12). *The 8 most common leadership styles & how to find your own* [Blog post]. Accessed at blog.hubspot.com/marketing/leadership-styles on May 18, 2021.

Berkowicz, J., & Myers, A. (2017, May 14). Trust in our schools requires honesty and good communication. *Education Week.* Accessed at blogs.edweek.org/edweek/leadership_360/2017/05 /trust_in_our_schools_requires_honesty_and_good_communication.html on December 8, 2020.

Bowen, J. (2018). *A model of effective goal-setting for leaders.* Accessed at https://3x5leadership.com /2018/07/05/a-model-of-effective-goal-setting-for-leaders on December 24, 2020.

BrainyQuote. (n.d.). *Ken Robinson quotes.* Accessed at www.brainyquote.com/quotes/ken _robinson_561885 on May 19, 2021.

Brown, B. (2018). *Dare to lead: Brave work, tough conversations, whole hearts.* New York: Random House.

Catmull, E. (2014). *Creativity, Inc.: Overcoming the unseen forces that stand in the way of true inspiration.* New York: Random House.

Center for Creative Leadership. (2020, November 24). *Adapting to change requires flexibility.* Accessed at www.ccl.org/articles/leading-effectively-articles/adaptability-1-idea-3-facts-5-tips on September 30, 2021.

Center for Creative Leadership. (2021, August 24). *Use active listening skills to coach others.* Accessed at www.ccl.org/articles/leading-effectively-articles/coaching-others-use-active-listening-skills on September 27, 2021.

Clark, J. T. (2019). *The impact of school culture upon an educational institution* [Applied research project, Cedarville University]. Accessed at https://digitalcommons.cedarville.edu/education _research_projects/9 on May 18, 2021.

Cleveland Clinic. (n.d.). *Communicate with H.E.A.R.T.®: Overview.* Accessed at https://my.cleveland clinic.org/departments/patient-experience/depts/experience-partners/licensed-programs /communicate-with-heart#overview-tab on December 3, 2020.

Comer, J. (1995). Lecture given at Education Service Center, Region IV. Houston, Texas.

Cone, T. (2019, March 22). *What is innovation leadership?* Accessed at https://medium.com /lightshed/what-is-innovation-leadership-8094f79620ca on May 18 2021.

Conzemius, A. E., & O'Neill, J. (2014). *The handbook for SMART school teams: Revitalizing best practices for collaboration* (2nd ed.). Bloomington, IN: Solution Tree Press.

Curtis, C. (2019, July 26). *Teacher role models: How to help students who need it most* [Blog post]. Accessed at https://online.campbellsville.edu/education/teacher-role-models on December 7, 2020.

D'Angelo, M. (2018, May 9). *Build a culture that increases employee retention.* Accessed at www.businessnewsdaily.com/8718-attracting-retaining-strategies.html on May 19, 2021.

Doran, G. T. (1981). There's a S.M.A.R.T. way to write management's goals and objectives. *Management Review, 70*(11), 35–36.

Dweck, C. S. (2006). *Mindset: The new psychology of success.* New York: Random House.

Dweck, C. S. (2015, September 22). Carol Dweck revisits the 'growth mindset'. *Education Week.* Accessed at www.edweek.org/leadership/opinion-carol-dweck-revisits-the-growth-mindset/2015 /09 on May 19, 2021.

Dweck, C. S. (2016, January 13). What having a "growth mindset" actually means. *Harvard Business Review.* Accessed at https://hbr.org/2016/01/what-having-a-growth-mindset-actually-means on May 18, 2021.

Eppinga, J., Salina, C., Girtz, S., & Martinez, D. (2018). *What's (relational) trust have to do with it?* Accessed at www.ascd.org/el/articles/whats-%28relational%29-trust-have-to-do-with-it on May 18, 2021.

Farnam Street. (2015). *Carol Dweck: A summary of growth and fixed mindsets* [Blog post]. Accessed at https://fs.blog/2015/03/carol-dweck-mindset on May 18, 2021.

Fullan, M. (2001). *Leading in a culture of change.* San Francisco: Jossey-Bass.

Fullan, M. (2008). *The six secrets of change: What the best leaders do to help their organizations survive and thrive.* San Francisco: Jossey-Bass.

Gagnon, D. (2019, February 8). *10 qualities of a good teacher.* Accessed at www.snhu.edu/about-us /newsroom/2017/12/qualities-of-a-good-teacher on May 18, 2021.

Goodwin, B. (2017, March 1). *Research matters / Personalization and failing forward.* Accessed at www.ascd.org/el/articles/personalization-and-failing-forward on May 18, 2021.

Goodwin, B., & Cameron, G. (2015). *Balanced leadership for powerful learning: Tools for achieving success in your school.* Association for Supervision and Curriculum Development.

Greenleaf, R. K. (1970). *The servant as leader.* Cambridge, MA: Center for Applied Studies.

Greenleaf, R. K. (2015). *The servant as leader* (Revised ed.). South Orange, NJ: The Greenleaf Center for Servant Leadership.

Griggs, B. (2016, January 4). *10 great quotes from Steve Jobs.* Accessed at www.cnn.com/2012/10/04 /tech/innovation/steve-jobs-quotes/index.html on May 19, 2021.

Henry, T. (2018). *Herding tigers: Be the leader that creative people need.* New York: Portfolio/Penguin.

Hereford, Z. (n.d.). *4 keys to good communication skills for workplace and life.* Accessed at www.essentiallifeskills.net/goodcommunicationskills.html on May 18, 2021.

Ho, L. (2018, September 26). *What is creativity? We all have it, and need it.* Accessed at www.lifehack.org/810923/what-is-creativity on January 24, 2021.

Houston Chronicle. (2021, May 19). *Is it important to be open minded in the workplace?* Accessed at https://work.chron.com/important-open-minded-workplace-6124.html on September 29, 2021.

Intuyu Consulting. (2017, May 6). *Ethical leadership and integrity.* Accessed at https://intuyu consulting.com.au/2017/06/05/ethical-leadership-and-integrity on December 3, 2020.

Knerl, L. (2019, March 12). *Three essential elements of educational leadership* [Blog post]. Accessed at www.northeastern.edu/graduate/blog/educational-leadership/#:~:text=Reiss%20Medwed%20 says%20that%20a%20personal%20commitment%20to,the%20authenticity%20to%20share%20 its%20value%20to%20others. on May 19, 2021.

Kwan, L. B. (2019). The collaboration blind spot. *Harvard Business Review.* Accessed at https://hbr .org/2019/03/the-collaboration-blind-spot on May 19, 2021.

Lathan, J. (n.d.). *10 traits of successful school leaders.* Accessed at https://onlinedegrees.sandiego.edu /effective-educational-leadership on May 18, 2021.

Lattimer, C. (2018, October 3). 5 characteristics of an open-minded leader. *The People Development Magazine.* Accessed at https://peopledevelopmentmagazine.com/2018/10/03/5-characteristics -open-minded-leader on September 27, 2020.

Llopis, G. (2014, April 7). 5 ways leaders enable innovation in their teams. *Forbes.* Accessed at www.forbes.com/sites/glennllopis/2014/04/07/5-ways-leaders-enable-innovation-in-their-teams /?sh=7ae7d7798c4c on December 31, 2020.

Lunenburg, F. C., & Irby, B. J. (2006). *The principalship: Vision to action.* Belmont, CA: Thomson/ Wadsworth.

Lynch, M. (2020, March 23). *Effective education leaders are flexible.* Accessed at www.theedadvocate .org/effective-education-leaders-are-flexible on November 9, 2020.

Maxwell, J. C. (2000). *Failing forward: Turning mistakes into stepping stones for success.* New York: HarperCollins.

Miller, P. (2012, February). Leadership communication: The three levels. *Today's Manager.* Accessed at www.mcgill.ca/engage/files/engage/leadership_communication_miller_2015.pdf on May 18, 2021.

Mind Tools Content Team. (n.d.). *Servant leadership: Putting your team first, and yourself second.* Accessed at www.mindtools.com/pages/article/servant-leadership.htm on May 19, 2021.

Mintz, S. (2018, March 6). *Leadership & ethics go hand in hand* [Blog post]. Accessed at www.ethicssage.com/2018/03/leadership-ethics-go-hand-in-hand.html on May 18, 2021.

Mulvahill, E. (2018, May 21). *What is genius hour and how can I try it in my classroom?* Accessed at www.weareteachers.com/what-is-genius-hour on May 18, 2021.

Murray, T. C., & Sheninger, E. C. (2018, March 16). *What it means to be a true leader* [Blog post]. Accessed at https://inservice.ascd.org/what-it-means-to-be-a-true-leader on May 18, 2021.

National Governors Association Center for Best Practices & Council of Chief State School Officers. (2010). *Common Core State Standards for English language arts and literacy in history/social studies, science, and technical subjects.* Washington, DC: Authors. Accessed at www.corestandards.org /assets/CCSSI_ELA%20Standards.pdf on September 30, 2021.

Newman, P. (2019, July 25). *5 ways to change & improve school climate & culture* [Blog post]. Accessed at www.kickboardforschools.com/blog/post/school-culture-climate/5-ways-to-change-improve -school-climate-culture/ on May 18, 2021.

O'Brien, A. (2016, June 9). *3-step method to increase teacher voice* [Blog post]. Accessed at www.edutopia.org/blog/increasing-teacher-voice-decision-making-anne-obrien on May 19, 2021.

Oxford Languages. (n.d.). Integrity. In *Google English dictionary*. Accessed at www.google.com /search?q=integrity&rlz=1C1CHBF_enUS872US872&oq=integrity&aqs=chrome..69i57j0i4 33i512j0i20i263i512j0i433i512j46i20i199i263i433i465i512j46i199i291i512j46i175i199i 512l2j46i131i175i199i433i512j46i199i291i512.1294j0j4&sourceid=chrome&ie=UTF-8 on September 30, 2021.

Page, L., & Brin, S. (2004). *2004 Founders' IPO letter: "An owner's manual" for Google shareholders.* Accessed at https://abc.xyz/investor/founders-letters/2004-ipo-letter on August 20, 2021.

Parrish, S., & Beaubien, R. (2018). *The great mental models: General thinking concepts* (Vol. 1). Ottawa, ON: Latticework.

Parrish, S., & Beaubien, R. (2019). *The great mental models: Physics, chemistry and biology* (Vol. 2). Ottawa, ON: Latticework.

Peterson-DeLuca, A. (2016, October 5). *Top 5 qualities of effective teachers, according to teachers* [Blog post]. Accessed at https://blog.savvas.com/top-5-qualities-of-effective-teachers-according-to-teachers on May 19, 2021.

Petrone, P. (2019, January 14). *Why collaboration breaks down—and how to avoid it* [Blog post]. Accessed at www.linkedin.com/business/learning/blog/productivity-tips/why-collaboration- breaks-down-and-how-to-avoid-it on April 20, 2020.

Positive Psychology Center. (2004). *Open-mindedness.* Accessed at www.authentichappiness.sas.upenn .edu/newsletters/authentichappinesscoaching/open-mindedness on September 29, 2021.

Price, D. (2019, December 15). *Innovation and organizational culture: How to foster innovative thinking and promote innovation in an organization.* Accessed at www.ckju.net/en/dossier /organizational-culture-and-freedom-fail-innovative-thinking-promote-innovation/1291 on May 19, 2021.

Price-Mitchell, M. (2015, June 9). *Creating a culture of integrity in the classroom* [Blog post]. Accessed at www.edutopia.org/blog/8-pathways-creating-culture-integrity-marilyn-price-mitchell on May 19, 2021.

Quaglia Institute for Student Aspirations, & Teacher Voice and Aspirations International Center. (2014). *Teacher voice report 2010–2014.* Accessed at www.sagepublications.com/images/eblast /CorwinPress/mcm/Quaglia%20Teacher%20Voice%20Report_final.pdf on May 19, 2021.

Raudys, J. (2020, July 31). *The 6 qualities of a good teacher (+25 ways to show them)* [Blog post]. Accessed at www.prodigygame.com/blog/qualities-of-a-good-teacher on May 19, 2021.

Rayner, L. (2020, September 14). *What is the relational leadership model?* Accessed at www.graduate program.org/2020/09/what-is-the-relational-leadership-model on November 9, 2020.

Robinson, J. (2013, May 16). *School leadership and 3 acts of integrity to practice today* [Blog post]. Accessed at https://the21stcenturyprincipal.blogspot.com/2013/05/school-leadership-and-3-acts -of.html on October 2, 2020.

Schaefer, B. (2015, October 12). *On becoming a leader: Building relationships and creating communities.* Accessed at https://er.educause.edu/articles/2015/10/on-becoming-a-leader-building -relationships-and-creating-communities on May 19, 2021.

Sheninger, E. C. (2016). *Uncommon learning: Creating schools that work for kids.* Thousand Oaks, CA: Corwin Press.

Sinek, S. (2009). *How great leaders inspire action* [Video file]. Accessed at www.ted.com/talks/simon _sinek_how_great_leaders_inspire_action?language=en on July 20, 2021.

Sinek, S. (2012, April 10). *How to talk about your weaknesses.* Accessed at https://blog.startwithwhy .com/refocus/2012/04/how-to-talk-about-your-weaknesses.html on September 30, 2021.

Smith, M. M. (2015, July 22). *6 ways the best leaders innovate and bring great ideas to life.* Accessed at www.tlnt.com/6-ways-the-best-leaders-innovate-and-bring-great-ideas-to-life on March 17, 2020.

South Carolina ASCD. (2019, September 16). *Continuing to shine the light on servant leadership* [Blog post]. Accessed at https://inservice.ascd.org/continuing-to-shine-the-light-on-servant-leadership on November 5, 2020.

Stobierski, T. (2019, October 7). *How to motivate employees: 5 data-backed tips for managers* [Blog post]. Accessed at www.northeastern.edu/graduate/blog/how-to-motivate-your-employees on May 19, 2021.

Taylor, J. (2014, June 2). *Strong leadership starts with your mindset* [Blog post]. Accessed at www.psychologytoday.com/us/blog/the-power-prime/201406/strong-leadership-starts-your -mindset on February 19, 2020.

Tomlinson, C. A. (2017). *How to differentiate instruction in academically diverse classrooms* (3rd ed.). Alexandria, VA: Association for Supervision and Curriculum Development.

Travis, T. A. (2017, October 8). *2 flexibility principles 4 principals* [Blog post]. Accessed at www.linkedin.com/pulse/2-flexibility-principles-4-principals-toby-a-travis-ed-d- on September 30, 2021.

Wagner, C. R. (2006). *The school leader's tool for assessing and improving school culture.* Accessed at www.mssaa.org/gen/mssaa_generated_bin/documents/basic_module/School_culture_triage.pdf on May 17, 2021.

Walker, T. (2019). A high school teacher scrapped homework. Here's what happened next. *NEA Today.* Accessed at www.nea.org/advocating-for-change/new-from-nea/high-school-teacher -scrapped-homework-heres-what-happened-next on July 20, 2021.

Webb, N. L. (2002). *Depth-of-knowledge levels for four content areas.* Accessed at http://ossucurr.pb works.com/w/file/fetch/49691156/Norm%20web%20dok%20by%20subject%20area.pdf on July 20, 2021.

Wiggins, G., & McTighe, J. (2005). *Understanding by design* (Expanded 2nd ed.). Alexandia, VA: Association for Supervision and Curriculum Development.

Wynn, S. C. (2019). *What research says about leadership styles and their implications for school climate and teacher job satisfaction* [Master's dissertation, Cedarville University]. Accessed at https://bit.ly /3y5Gqqe on May 19, 2021.

Index

The Deliberate and Courageous Principal
Rhonda J. Roos

Fully step into your power as a school principal. By diving deep into five essential leadership actions and five essential leadership skills, you will learn how to grow in your role and accomplish incredible outcomes for your students and staff.
BKG013

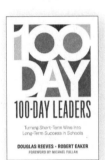

100-Day Leaders
Douglas Reeves and Robert Eaker

Within 100 days, schools can dramatically increase student achievement, transform faculty morale, reduce discipline issues, and much more. Using *100-Day Leaders* as a guide, you will learn how to achieve a series of short-term wins that combine to form long-term success.
BKF919

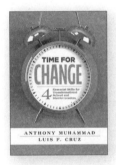

Time for Change
Anthony Muhammad and Luis F. Cruz

Exceptional leaders have four distinctive skills: strong communication, the ability to build trust, the ability to increase the skills of those they lead, and a results orientation. *Time for Change* offers powerful guidance for those seeking to develop and strengthen these skills.
BKF683

Holistic Leadership, Thriving Schools
Jane A. G. Kise

Build a school where students flourish academically while getting their needs met socially, physically, and emotionally. With this practical guide, school leaders will discover a toolkit of strategies for navigating competing priorities and uniting their school communities around one common purpose: supporting the whole child.
BKF821

Solution Tree | Press a division of
Solution Tree

Visit SolutionTree.com or call 800.733.6786 to order.

Wait! Your professional development journey doesn't have to end with the last pages of this book.

We realize improving student learning doesn't happen overnight. And your school or district shouldn't be left to puzzle out all the details of this process alone.

No matter where you are on the journey, we're committed to helping you get to the next stage.

Take advantage of everything from **custom workshops** to **keynote presentations** and **interactive web and video conferencing**. We can even help you develop an action plan tailored to fit your specific needs.

Let's get the conversation started.

Call 888.763.9045 today.

SolutionTree.com